THE GLOBAL DESI

THE GLOBAL DESI

REFLECTIONS ON HOME AND AWAY

SUNDEEP BHUTORIA

MACMILLAN

First published 2021 by Macmillan
an imprint of Pan Macmillan Publishing India Private Limited
707, Kailash Building
26, KG Marg
New Delhi – 110 001
www.panmacmillan.co.in

Pan Macmillan, The Smithson, 6 Briset Street, London EC1M 5NR
Associated companies throughout the world
www.panmacmillan.com

ISBN 978-93-90742-31-8

1 3 5 7 9 8 6 4 2

Typeset in Cambria by Allcap Communications

Printed and bound in India by Anderson Printing House, Kolkata

You can take the man out of India but you won't get India out of him. Sundeep Bhutoria does not travel to sample the cuisines of the world but lives like an Indian around the world. What a life! He visits countries to check out how much they can bring India home to him. Here you can share with him delectable dishes from India in Rio or Singapore or Seoul. It is a joy to read how he finds the best Indian anywhere and everywhere he goes. But then he is one of the best himself. From his keen observations on social issues and eye for detail it is evident that he is a concerned citizen.

— Lord Meghnad Desai

I

Travel & Food

II

Social Issues

III

Literature

Contents

Foreword

In September 2016, I was invited to the Vatican for the canonisation of Mother Teresa. It was there that I probably had my most memorable time with Sundeep Bhutoria. We were staying in the same hotel, and to meet someone from my country — that too someone that I knew so well — so far away from home, was wonderfully reassuring. Sundeep, as usual, had organised a sumptuous dinner with the who's who of Rome and the Vatican City in attendance. It was another example of how whatever Sundeep does, he does it *shaan se*!

I have known Sundeep for 25 years now, during which time we have developed a seamless professional relationship as well as a deep personal bond. Sundeep is one of those friends with whom you can pick up from where you left off. Impeccably dressed, incurably passionate about his projects, and possessing that unteachable touch of class, he is a thorough gentleman. He keeps a beautiful home, loves his food and travel, and is always keen to do something or the other that enhances culture for the benefit of his native Kolkata.

Sundeep's writings encapsulate his best qualities — cultural consciousness, curiosity for and acceptance of diversity, and above all, an unbreakable connection to his roots. These are also the qualities that make him a quintessential "global desi".

Having made Kolkata my *karmabhumi*, I have seen how the city has grown and evolved over the decades. For me, Kolkata is, and will forever remain, magical — a mesmerising city that knows how to share and get the best out of its inhabitants. The presence of people like Sundeep have ensured that Kolkata carries on with its rich legacy of cultural cosmopolitanism, as a place that never fails to open its heart for those eager to experience its charms.

At the same time, it devastates me when I see the levels of poverty and deprivation on the streets of Kolkata. I am glad that as a cultural commentator, these sordid aspects of our civilisation do not escape the notice of Sundeep, who has never shied away from addressing issues of social relevance in his work.

During my travels around the world, I have seen the architecture of Kolkata reflected in several corners of London; I have seen Italians live life with the same verve and enthusiasm as so many Calcuttans do; I have seen people of Indian origin in Kenya and South Africa celebrate our cultural norms with as much dedication as people back home. My journeys across the globe have reiterated my faith and my love for Indianness, and it gives me great pleasure to encounter that same faith and love in this beautifully crafted book by Sundeep.

The last year has been tough on all of us. The pandemic has shown us that every industry is vulnerable, not least my industry of entertainment. It is my sincere hope that, alongside the stellar endeavours he is already engaged in, Sundeep also spearheads the integration of technology and culture in the time to come, so that more virtual events can be organised, unaffected by the problems posed by Covid-19.

The sky is the limit for Sundeep, and given his vision, adaptability, and perseverance, I am certain that he has a whole lot more left to achieve. *The Global Desi: Reflections on Home and Away* is not just a compelling account of what Sundeep stands for; it is also a celebration of the values that make our culture one of the oldest and most glorious cultures known to humankind.

I am sure you will thoroughly enjoy this book, just as I have, and dwell on the multifarious insights that underline the very best the world has to offer through a uniquely Indian lens.

Usha Uthup
Kolkata
March 2021

Preface

Many years back, I was in the South Korean city of Incheon, just before it became a destination for international conventions. While one brings back many memories from every trip — and my work and passions have taken me all over the globe, including many unknown places many have never heard of — the most abiding memory from my maiden visit to Incheon was near-starvation!

Being a vegetarian, my gastronomic options are often quite limited in foreign shores, but in Incheon, it seemed as though the very concept of vegetarian food did not exist at that time. I survived on Korean rice and tomato puree for the entire duration of my stay.

So, you can imagine the relish with which I fell upon the humble *dal-chawal* and paneer that I was served by an Indian restaurant in Seoul, which was my destination after Incheon. Though not the best in the business, to my hungry soul, this home food tasted nothing short of the proverbial manna from heaven.

I enjoy my travels immensely, especially discovering new cultures and interacting with different kinds of people. Oh yes, I even enjoy the misadventures! They, after all, make for the best stories later. As much as I love to fly off to far-flung destinations, I always carry India in my heart wherever I go, and look for a little bit of India in every new place I visit. I make it a point to try out new places serving Indian food or look up old favourites that have served me well in the past. Connecting with NRIs is always on my agenda on overseas trips. I meet up with Indian chefs making a mark in the international culinary scene, enquire into how the Indian community is faring or how the lives of Indian expats are shaping up abroad.

These experiences and interactions have led me to write columns for different newspapers and my own blogs for over a decade, sharing with readers my myriad anecdotes and some observations about social issues that affect all our lives. I was encouraged by several men and women of letters, and many friends, to compile these pieces into a book.

Having thoroughly enjoyed the publication of *Calcuttascape: Musings of a Globetrotter* last year and its exceptionally warm reception in all quarters, I have put together another compilation of articles and blogs, titled 'The Global Desi: Reflections on Home and Away'.

'The Global Desi', which focuses on three topics very close to my heart — food & travel, literature and social issues — is my small way of celebrating India at home and abroad, at the same time also highlighting some issues around us that demand our attention. The articles have been written over several years but each of them addresses a topic that is universal and timeless. Based on the feedback I received for *Calcuttascape*, I have mentioned the publication where each article appeared and the date so that readers can relate to the time and context of each article.

With my close ties to Rajasthan, I have had the privilege of a ringside view of one of the greatest literary events in the world — Jaipur Literature Festival — right from its inception in 2006. Being an avid reader and having an interest in writing myself, I have witnessed with great pride and delight how the Pink City has become a shining beacon of literary celebration, one that draws writers and readers, thinkers and leaders from every part of the world. My love for JLF, however, has not blinded me to some aspects that could be improved, which I have raised in my columns as well.

The social issues addressed in my columns are based on what I see around me and how I feel about certain norms and practices. While I believe that being Indian is a unique privilege in many ways, there are two things about us that leave me disappointed, often angry. One is our complete apathy towards injustice done to others, and the second is our reluctance to follow up on any vexing issue once our own work is done, be it a passport issue or a matter of consumer rights.

But these problems continue to plague us, which is probably why I received the most enthusiastic feedback on those articles in *Calcuttascape* that raised some pertinent questions for public good. I have included a few of those articles in this book as well, for I feel very strongly that the only way to right the wrongs happening around us is to keep asking the uncomfortable questions and demanding accountability.

I would like to thank all the editors who have believed in my ideas and my writing, providing me with a platform to connect with a wide array of readers across the country and beyond. I have always treated the printed word with the greatest reverence, I do hope I have been able to do justice to their faith in me.

I would like to express my sincere gratitude to Smt. Usha Uthup, who has very kindly penned the Foreword for this book. It is because of the encouragement of such stalwarts that I continue to write and share my thoughts with the world.

And finally, dear reader, a big Thank You to you, for picking up this book and giving it the gift of your time.

Sundeep Bhutoria

Kolkata

April 2021

Travel & Food

Dedicated to

My native place, ***Sujangarh****,*
where it all began

Meals make the society, hold the fabric together in lots of ways that were charming and interesting and intoxicating to me. The perfect meal, or the best meals, occur in a context that frequently has very little to do with the food itself.

— Anthony Bourdain

1

The 'Fall' Guy

It was the last week of August when Halim *saab* (Hashim Abdul Halim, Speaker of the West Bengal Assembly) gave me a call asking whether I would like to attend the Commonwealth Parliamentary Association (CPA)'s Millennium Youth Parliament at Manchester in November. Having attended a UN Youth Conference in Luxembourg and an International Youth Convention in Greece earlier, I jumped at the idea. But I also told Halim *saab*, the president of CPA's West Bengal branch, that I would be dependent on him for a detailed briefing of what it was all about. Over the past few months, as I started corresponding with the CPA, I began to realise how huge the event would be. But nothing could quite prepare me for the real thing, bringing together 111 young delegates from 108 countries....

November 20: The fact that this trip would be an exception to the rule was clear from the start with the British Airways flight a 'record' 3 hours and 20 minutes late! I reached London in the late evening and immediately got in touch with Mahbub Alam and Raja Gomez at the CPA headquarters, who asked me to meet them over lunch the next day.

November 21: I left St. James' Court and headed straight for Westminster House. Once I had passed through the forbidding security corridor, a warm welcome awaited me. Over a lengthy lunch at the canteen, Mahbub Alam, Sarwar Jamal Nizam, an MP from Bangladesh, Meenakshi Dhar, a Kashmiri lady related to the Nehru family and presently with the CPA, and I discussed everything from Kashmir to the Bush-Gore stalemate.

November 22: Sharp at 10am, I turned up at the House of Lords. Emmy, from the CPA, was there to take me around. Despite the grandeur and the decorum, what endures about my visit is the disappointment of missing Tony Blair's Q&A slated for the afternoon, as I had to rush for our welcome lunch at the Royal Commonwealth Society Hall.

It looked like an invasion by a youth army gathered from all corners of the world. After mingling with fellow delegates from Australia and Anguilla, Zambia and Zimbabwe, I finally caught up with my fellow Indians — Nivedith Thomas Alva (son of Margaret Alva) and Raghuvendra Mirdha (grandson of Ram Nivas Mirdha). Diplomats from all countries with a presence in London turned up for the occasion, but India House was conspicuous by its absence. After lunch, we were off to Manchester on a Virgin train.

Once at the Jurys Inn hotel, it was time to get down to business. We were immediately divided up along political lines — Youth Party (YP), New Millennium Party (NMP), Direct Democracy Party (DDP) and two independents — for two separate dinner briefings. We were informed that the YP would be the government, the NMP the chief Opposition and the DDP the other Opposition party.

Nivedith and I were in the NMP. We were given 40 minutes to select a Leader of the Opposition and six shadow ministers. Steered by two British girls, Samantha and Sharon, secretaries to two MPs in the House of Commons, we went into vote mode, and Sam Moreton, the president of the New South Wales Young Australian Labour Party, beat me to the leader's post by two votes (it was only then that I noticed the large Australian contingent in the party!). I, however, was unanimously elected to the post of shadow home affairs minister. With the power play out of the way, we chalked out our parliamentary strategy. Later in the evening, we learnt that Crios Freeman of St. Kitts & Nevis was the Youth Party's Prime Minister and Leah Radcliffe, from Australia, the leader of the DDP (of which Mirdha was a member).

The dos (good behaviour, blazer and tie...) and don'ts

(disrespect shown to the Speaker, jeans...) were clearly laid out at the dinner table.

November 23: There was a real buzz in the frosty morning air (the temperature hovering around zero degrees) as we left for the House of Commons Chamber, Granada Studios. It was quintessentially Westminster — everything from the ornate to the officialese. The morning session saw the welcome address by CPA secretary-general Arthur Donahue, the Speakers' procession, and the Throne Speech by Commonwealth secretary-general Donald McKinnon.

After lunch, the parliamentary proceedings got underway — the Opposition motion on compulsory and free education for everyone till the age of 16 and the adjournment debates on programmes for poverty reduction, literacy and disability. Amidst deliberation and debate, there were some memorable parliamentary moments. Isodoro Charles Galvez from Belize brought the House down with a 'point of order', which Speaker Baroness Fookes of Plymouth admitted as 'most pertinent', concerning a dictionary being provided to all members in order to follow the eloquence of a girl from Australia, Melissa Gaddie of Victoria. Physically challenged herself, Melissa moved many to tears with her impassioned plea for the rights of the disabled.

The proceedings came to an end just as things were

getting interesting. On my way back to the hotel, I suddenly thought, 'Why not do something really different, like bringing the government down?' After some quick calculations, I realised that it was definitely doable!

My first target, Leah Ratcliffe. I went pub-hopping, trying desperately to track her down. I finally found her and came straight to the point: 'Let's bring the government down.'

'Can we?' she shot back.

I explained the numbers game to her (NMP + DDP > YP) to prove that we could. But she refused to 'take the risk'. Then I discussed the matter with some of my party members, who seemed excited, yet sceptical, at the prospect. We finally decided to hold a special meeting early next morning to work out our plan of action.

November 24: The big day dawned cold and cloudy. At a pre-breakfast meeting, we decided to 'take it as it comes'. Back in Parliament by 8.30am. After the Speaker's procession, the debate on the Bill to lower the voting age from 18 to 14 began. The stage was set for the sparks to fly. Debate led to drama, with the Prime Minister being forced to offer a 'public apology' after I pointed out that he had contradicted his party manifesto.

With time ticking, I was getting restive, looking for the 'right' moment. It came during the Committee of the

Whole House when I exhorted our leader to declare that this 'chamber has no confidence in the government'.

This really set a wild cat among the prim and proper pigeons in Parliament. The CPA secretariat went into a huddle to discuss this unprecedented turn of events. Finally, the Speaker decided that this extraordinary situation would be resolved by a hand vote.

Seeing the confusion in the DDP ranks, I quickly crossed over to their benches. 'What do you want for supporting us?' I asked Leah. After some deliberation with her leaders, she said: 'The deputy prime minister's post and two shadow ministers.'

Done.

Up went all the NMP and most DDP hands (a few Africans held back as they did not want an African PM replaced by an Australian). Down came the government.

The jubilation in our camp was matched by the shock in the government, and even the organisers', ranks.

A member of the Youth Party cried foul: A no-confidence could not be admitted during a debate on a Bill, by Westminster rules. Clerk Shona McGlashan (who's also the clerk at the House of Commons) forwarded the point to the Speaker. But the Baroness decided to go by the practice in 'most parliaments of the Commonwealth countries', and not just the UK.

A question time, Canadian-style (any minister can be asked anything), was scheduled for the post-lunch session. By then, the shock had given way to outrage. The oakwood panels reverberated with cries of 'shame, shame; cheaters, cheaters' as the DDP bore the brunt of the attack for 'selling out' to us. The Speaker had to intervene six times and, finally, threatened to call in the Sergeant of Arms before order was restored. I was enjoying every moment of it. And you thought such parliamentary disorder only happens in India!

By the time the House rose for the last time, the spirit of the Commonwealth had prevailed. Political differences buried in-Parliament, we all trooped out. After a civic dinner at the magnificent Manchester Town Hall, hosted by the mayor, we finally broke free. Ties tossed aside, we all went pub crawling till the early hours of Saturday. I probably had the most fun as I don't drink!

November 25: Farewell time. After an experience of a lifetime and making 'friends with the future', I headed back home.

Although I wonder exactly where all of us will be five years from now, I'm sure many will help shape their states' political destinies.

The Telegraph, Kolkata
December 1, 2000

2

The Rails Still Roll

It is 3pm and I am Jaipur-bound on the Jodhpur-Puri Express. This is my first train ride in 15 years. Since morning, I have been thinking of cancelling my train ticket and opting for an alternative; but there's no flight from Jodhpur to Jaipur, and a detour via Delhi takes almost nine hours, including transit. By road, it takes around five to six hours, as does this train.

Somewhat reluctantly, I decide to stick to the train. I am the only one in the AC First Class compartment, with only a few others in the rest of the train when it starts. As the train moves, I stare out of the window... into my past.

As a boy, I used to frequently travel from my paternal grandfather's home in Churu to my maternal grandfather's place in Sujangarh on the local train, covering 110 kilometres.

It would be very crowded, with hundreds of passengers crammed into a bogey meant for not more than 70! My co-passengers at times included goats and other four-legged beings. Counting trees from the moving train was my favourite pastime.

It seems the wheels of time move rather slowly for the Great Indian Railways — nothing much has changed since my childhood. Despite some of the modern trappings, the spirit remains the same. At Jodhpur station, I had noticed three metal detectors at the entrance. Not a single one was working and no one cared to pass through them.

But, of course, in the last 15 years there have been some add-ons. I see there is a reading light, but no bulb. There is a tissue holder in the toilet, but no tissues. There is a dustbin, which is filled to the brim. There is a cupboard with a hanger rod, but no hangers to put clothes on.

The toilet-in-use indicator always glows red. The dining room staff is very well uniformed, but the teapots they serve us in are cracked and the tea barely warm. The same typed chart remains pasted to the door in the same unfriendly print.

There is an old saying: 'If you want to see the real India, you must travel by rail.' It still holds good.

There used to be theft of bulbs and other items from Indian trains and that continues unabated. The state of our trains is indicative of the state of our nation. We are as uncaring about public property as we used to be, but we still blame the government for everything.

Sundeep Roves, DNA, Jaipur

September 2, 2012

3

Upscale NYC... and Pedicab Views

That weekend, the New York weather was perfect for a stroll. I took a long walk towards the south of Central Park and, after a cup of spicy tea at the Taj Group-owned Pierre Hotel lounge, I decided to take a pedicab ride.

Pedicabs, an utterly unconventional mode of transport in New York City, are a smarter version of our rickshaws and a great way to travel through Central Park, since they are open on all sides and you get a 360-degree view around you. It has a collapsible canopy, which comes in handy in case it rains or the sun is too stark. The pedicab drivers often fill in as tour guides and interpreters.

I was really lucky to get a driver who seemed very intelligent and informed. He told me that the Upper West Side (UWS) of the Park was teeming with celeb residents like Madonna, LeBron James, Steven Spielberg, Demi Moore, Bruce Willis, Michael Douglas, Matt Damon, Tiger Woods, Steve Martin and others.

While the Upper East Side (UES) of the Park, the toniest of tony areas, belongs to the Rockefellers, Kennedys, Vanderbilts, Astors, Whitneys and other old-moneyed families often linked to the great American success story, with old mansions and grand pre-War houses. Once known as the 'Silk Stocking District', it still is one of the most affluent neighbourhoods of New York City, with the most expensive real estate in the world. The famous Met (Metropolitan Museum of Art) is located here.

My guide helped me espy the famous $88 million penthouse that a Russian millionaire had bought for his 22-year-old daughter studying in New York University. Dmitry E. Rybolovlev's 15 Central Park West penthouse condo created history as the most expensive residential deal in Manhattan last year.

I asked my guide what he used to do earlier. It took some more conversation and small talk before he opened up. He said he had been a professor of English literature in Burkina Faso, West Africa. Even more surprising to me was the fact that he had got his Green Card in a lottery.

He told me that the US government conducts an online lottery from time to time, and if you win, you approach them and get your Green Card. I found out later that he was right. The US government indeed has such an online system in place. However, one has to be careful to avoid numerous fake sites.

The professor doesn't want his family or students back home to know that he is a pedicab driver in New York. I promised not to write his name.

We know very well what many Indians do to get a Green Card. Many of them work jobs they are not comfortable telling their families and friends about. During my extensive travels overseas, I get a fair idea of the sacrifices people make just to have that blue passport or the Green Card. Many of them can be seen sitting across the nine thousand benches of Central Park.

Post-Independence, haven't many village boys shifted to cities, ensnared by the glamour and ended up being *rickshawallahs* in the lanes of those cities?

Sundeep Roves, DNA, Jaipur

September 30, 2012

4

Little Indias, All over London

London has always been Bollywood's favourite destination for holidaying and shopping. The city is also home to some of the best restaurants that offer a stunning variety of global cuisines.

During my recent visit to London, I finally managed to get a table at the Kai Mayfair. Having missed out on two earlier occasions, I took no chances and booked in advance at the 'most premium' Chinese restaurant in London. Their specialty — classical authentic Chinese dishes and modern Chinese fusion food.

The fact that the Bachchan, Khan and Roshan families are often seen at Kai adds to its reputation as a hotspot. They say if you want to meet KJo (Karan Johar) in London, visit Kai.

During the summer, many politicians, often very touchy about China and Chinese policies, make a beeline here. Rumour has it that many from the Bollywood brigade have condos close by. This restaurant also sells wines from different regions of the world, including one from the Château Pétrus in the Bordeaux region of France that costs £3,000.

There are many other places that have their own pull. A small restaurant on Church Street called Lahori Tandoori — a franchise of the famous original Lahori in East London — serves mouth-watering kebabs, rolls, *sheesha* and masala chai. Again, a great address for Bollywood stargazing. The roll call — Saif Ali Khan, Ajay Devgn, Shahid Kapoor and so on.

For those whose hearts beat for street food, Masala Zone, and its 10 outlets in London, is the right spot. From *jhaal muri* and *pav bhaji* to you name it, you will get it all! Masala Zone is a must-visit for Om Puri. Girish Karnad, too, dined here on his last visit.

Veeraswamy, with its quintessential Indian ambience, Warli paintings on the walls et al, is also here. It is said that the story of the first restaurant of Indian food started here. It made its mark first among Indians and later, especially its thalis, gained popularity with other Asian and British foodies.

Sitaaray in Drury Lane, Covent Garden, is famous for its kebab platters. It casts a Bollywood aura through its display of some very old and stunning signed photos of stars and film posters.

Apart from the Italian restaurant where Shah Rukh Khan dines, Indali Lounge is the latest addition to Baker Street. This one is all about healthy food and wise dining. The owner, Dr Lalwani, personally instructs his chefs and proudly offers butter chicken with no butter! Rest assured it is very tasty. Recently, the reading session of Javed Akhtar's latest book, *Lava*, took place here. Former British Prime Minister Tony Blair spoke at a charity evening here, too. The venue was used as a location in the club scene for Sangeeta Datta's *Life Goes On*, and the popular *River Song* was also filmed here.

There has been a sea change since 1921, when the first Indian food joints sprung up in London. Some of the fancy Indian restaurants, like Benares, Tamarind or Green Mint, cater to the English palate first. A new joint that has come up in Bryanston Street is called La Porte des Indes, whose Sunday brunches — with live jazz — are very popular.

The only Rajasthani restaurant in London, Chai Pani on Seymour Street, has closed down. But then Roti Chai opened on August 15 last year, which is close to another popular London destination — Selfridges and Marks & Spencer — a must-visit for Jaipurites visiting London.

To add to the variety, St. James' Crowne Plaza Hotel, by the Taj Group, is coming up with a new Bollywood suite, which would be dedicated to 100 years of Indian cinema.

To be priced at £5,100 a day, the suite is expected to be opened sometime in January 2013.

In the words of Prabhat Verma, general manager, St. James', you don't miss India in London. Quite true.

Sundeep Roves, DNA, Jaipur

October 21, 2012

5

First Time in Rio

Hotel Royal Tulip, Rio de Janeiro, Brazil: A spectacular aerial view, and it was love at first sight. Rio casts a spell on millions and I was no exception. I was in Rio for the 40th plenary of the World Federation of United Nations Associations (WFUNA). I checked in at Hotel Royal Tulip, which was formerly known as Intercontinental Rio.

Rio, already a hot tourist destination, has recently emerged as one of the new centres of the world for hosting conferences. For Indians and those who speak only English, Rio poses a problem. Without a working knowledge of Portuguese or at least a little bit of Spanish, you're in for a trying time communicating with the locals and finding your way around.

Rio sprang quite a few surprises. First, not a single English daily is published locally. Second, in this hi-tech communication era, you cannot buy a prepaid SIM for your mobile phone without a local social security number or citizenship documents.

My Indian cell phone could only receive text messages, but my attempts to send any proved futile. I was told there were different codes for different mobile networks and the standard international outgoing code did not work. Strangely, texts to London and US numbers worked just fine.

Rio, with its sun-lashed beaches, mountains, seas, islands, rain forests, waterfalls, promenades and stunning landscapes, is indeed one of the most picturesque cities in the world.

On Sundays, the sea front is a sea of humanity. Umbrellas spread like specks of colourful dots on a sandy canvas, stretching as far as the eye can see. Being on the beach is Rio's way of relaxing.

At noon, I went to one of the city's famous Portuguese restaurants called Antiquarius in the Leblon area; one of the poshest in the whole of Rio. There was an impressive array of starters but I, being a veggie, managed with tomato soup and salad.

It is really surprising that a city of nearly 13 million has no Indian restaurant. In all, there are some 25-odd Indian families in Rio, who keep in touch with one another. The close-knit Indian families had organised a cultural evening for us that began with Diwali prayers by the children, followed by a Kathak performance by three Brazilian artistes, a dance performance by Indians and finally some *dandiya, ghoomar* and fireworks by the beach.

Rio has countless attractions, but I say the famous steps of Escadaria Selarón, in the Lapa and Santa Teresa neighbourhood, is a must-see. It is a work of art by Chilean-born artist Jorge Selarón, who started renovating the dilapidated steps in 1990 by putting different shapes of blue, green and yellow tiles — the colours of the Brazilian flag. He also used ceramics and mirrors besides accepting tiles from all over the world.

I saw, near the starting point, tiles with pictures of Indian gods, which I captured on my camera. There are 250 steps measuring 125 metres, which are covered with over 2,000 tiles collected from more than 60 countries around the world.

Another tip is that one must try out the guarana drink — an extract from a local fruit famed for its stimulating effects. Guarana is also available in cans like Coke and in different flavours. It is very refreshing and energetic. Some people swear it improves cognitive skills.

Sundeep Roves, DNA, Jaipur

November 18, 2012

6

Brunch in Bangalore

Recently, I was in Bangalore and went to the ITC Gardenia for dinner. Again, I had the feeling (I had stayed in this green luxury hotel last year) that nature did not stop at the hotel's entrance, but came all the way in and, in fact, went all the way up to the upper storeys! All thanks to architect Rajinder Kumar and landscape artists Francesca and Patrick.

My good old friend and the hotel's general manager, Ranvir Bhandari, and his wife Danijela Radonic Bhandari, had invited me over for dinner once they came to know that I was in the city. Ranvir had been GM of ITC Sonar in Kolkata and has recently joined as vice-president, South.

The hotel's interiors have been created by Francesca Basu in a manner that portrays nature in all its hues and manifestations. 'Nature and its myriad life forms' is the theme that runs through each floor and room. Four vertical gardens show off a collection of 1,500 plants. The 'Living Wall' at The Cubbon Pavilion covers an entire section and has around 25,000 plants, reaching 30 metres up to the 12th floor, where daylight filters in to create an atrium effect. Much of Gardenia's lighting needs are met from natural sources. Over 1,200 species of philodendrons brought in from the Nilgiris now thrive indoors. The hotel also has an elevated heliport on the 22nd floor!

ITC Gardenia happens to be the first hotel in India to create the concept of 'vertical gardens' or 'vertical wall of plants' designed by French botanist Patrick Blanc, who has been inspired by the rainforests, especially the ability and adaptability of plants that vie for sunlight. Blanc has balanced the needs of soil, water and sunlight to create the lush resplendent indoor gardens that rise up from the open lobby to the ceilings high above.

We had dinner at Gardenia's West View Restaurant, where a new Italian chef has joined recently. The idea is to develop a complete Italian cuisine restaurant, Ranvir informed me. The new Italian chef was good and he had prepared a sumptuous vegetarian spread for us. Ranvir and I have a lot of common friends in Kolkata and we chatted about the past and things in general about Bengal and Kolkata.

***

It was a Sunday afternoon in Bangalore, and we were at a brunch to celebrate my cousin Anil Kathotia's birthday that went on till 8.30pm. By the time we actually called it a day, it was half-past 10! I think this is the longest brunch I have ever attended.

In recent years, Bangalore has developed the culture of day parties since there is a ban by law on liquor at late-night parties.

In the past five years, I have attended these brunches or lunch parties at the Blue Bar at Taj West End and once at the Gateway Taj Hotel, where the lunch lasted till almost 6pm.

At the Sunday party by the Windsor poolside, almost one-third of the guests picked up plates for the main course after 6pm! Till then, since 1.30pm actually, it had all been about bands, DJs, starters and live counters.

So, the next time you attend a brunch in Bangalore, you may be only a few hours away from your next day's lunch!

Sundeep Roves, DNA, Jaipur

December 16, 2012

7

Water by any Other Colour

I was in Delhi's ITC Maurya Sheraton on the Xmas weekend. A dense cover of fog in Delhi caused major chaos, with trains and planes getting fogged in. Thousands of travel plans went haywire and schedules got all scrambled.

The Maurya Sheraton had one extra cover — and a heavy security one at that — for Russian President Vladimir Putin, who was staying there from December 22 to 25, 2012.

Regulars know that the hotel hosts many foreign heads of state on their visits to India. It, in fact, had hosted five heads of state in the 10 days around Christmas, including Waddaulah ibni Al-Marhum of Brunei, Malaysian First Lady Datin Seri Hajah Rosmah binti Mansor, Laotian PM Thongsing Thammavong, and Singapore PM Lee Hsien Loong.

I have never been very fond of this property, finding it a tad loud. I often wonder when they get the time to clean up their coffee shops, given the endless stream of guests round the clock. Getting a table at the Bukhara on the same day is like a dream come true.

All other cities with ITC properties serve as my temporary residences during visits. Delhi is the only exception. I mostly prefer to stay at the India International Centre (IIC) if the stay is a long one. For visits spanning a day or two, I put up at the Hyatt Regency.

Recently, Anil Chadha took over as the GM of this flagship Maurya property of the ITC group. He is well known on the hotel circuit for his flair and efficiency in getting things done. He has an eye for the minutest of details. His qualities are contagious and seem to be catching up with the rank and file of the hotel.

There has been a perceptibly positive change in the quality of service since Chadha took charge, and I am now finally beginning to think that Maurya's fabled service extends beyond the heads of state to all who stay there. That's the reason I have once again an ITC property as my address in the capital on my visits there.

While in the coffee shop, I noticed some beautiful and elegant bottles on the side tables. The contrasting colours — red, blue, green — of the translucent bottles attracted me. I inquired about them and was told that these were portable water bottles introduced by Mr Chadha.

It sure caught my fancy and I immediately cancelled

my request for the conventional water bottle and asked for one of the elegant, coloured ones. I noticed all the bottles had a tag saying what the colours meant. The green one read: 'The colour green is regarded as a colour of accord and harmony.' The other bottles carried their own colourful messages.

In the past 20 years, there has been a sort of revolution in packaged or portable water in India. I remember the first time I flew overseas in 1994, and the Aeroflot air hostess asked me whether I would take gas water or mineral water. I had no answer. I wonder how many people, even today, know the difference between mineral water and bottled water or drinking water. In fact, how well do we know the difference between Himalaya and Evian even though both are tagged as mineral water?

For the past couple of years, premium hotels in India have begun stocking gas water. In fact, Jaipur's Marriott has a couple of options of mineral water for premium brands.

It seems some revolutionary changes are upon us in the drinking water segment in India. Looks like the great marketing minds have detected a multi-million dollar enterprise around the simple act of quenching our thirst!

Sundeep Roves, DNA, Jaipur

February 2, 2013

8

Curries of New York

My love for desi food is such that even while travelling abroad, the first thing that I look for is Indian restaurants. My travels in the West have acquainted me with all restaurants that have good Indian food to offer. In the process, I have made friends with several chefs, owners and waiters.

In New York, Lexington Avenue has numerous Indian eateries. In Long Island, Murray Hill is commonly termed as 'Curry Hill' because of the presence of a large number of Indian restaurants — including Curry in Hurry, Chote Nawab, Handi, Tawa, Dhaba, Food of India, Bhatti, Bhojan, Madras Mahal, Vatan, Pongal, Mint and Copper Chimney. The newer restaurants that have been there for three or four years are Tulsi and Junoon. The latter is bigger and has an attractive décor, but I was a little disappointed with the food.

Tulsi, according to me, is one of the finest contemporary Indian restaurants. When I first went there a few years ago,

Hemant Mathur, the chef-in-charge, was looking after its kitchen. After tasting the food, I thought he deserved the 'Best Chef's Crown'; whether it was tandoor or mocktails, it was simply lip-smacking.

The niche that Tulsi has carved out can be measured by the presence of eminent customers like UN Secretary-General Ban Ki-moon, Indra Nooyi, Salman Rushdie and Woody Allen, among others. The place was awarded Michelin star status that chefs across the world consider the ultimate accolade. I myself had invited a Head of State there for lunch knowing his taste for Indian food.

Two other Indian restaurants — Junoon and Tamarind Tribeca — have also won the coveted status. This indicates the rising popularity of desi food in the West. Tamarind Tribeca is a big restaurant and serves Indian fusion food, worth trying for its deliciousness and ambience.

Recently, when I went to New York in September, I ordered some food from Darbar. The next day I went to Tulsi but I found that the food had started to taste different. I asked for one of the restaurant managers, Mr Prakash, and was informed that Prakash was on leave and that Hemant is no longer associated with Tulsi. He had left Tulsi for another venture.

In the evening, one of the United Nations Association (UNA) officials invited me — knowing well my love for

Indian food — to an Indian outlet with a fancy name, Malai Marke. The restaurant is located on 318E 6 Street. Among the many Indian eateries that have sprung up on this street, only Malai Marke was fully occupied on a Monday evening.

I also realised the restaurant caters to the Western palate. The food was basic in taste, especially the vegetarian dishes. I came to know from my host that it was largely because of its excellent non-vegetarian cuisine that the restaurant was favoured by non-Indians, even on a Monday evening.

Lexington 29th Street — known as Curry Hill — has seen many Indian and Pakistani restaurants come up in the last 10 years or so. Once, after parking the car and taking the sidewalk towards Lucky Paan, I suddenly saw the board of a restaurant called Haldi. I recalled that during my meeting with Ramu Damodaran, senior official, United Nations, he had mentioned that chef Hemant Mathur was associated with Haldi now. Soon, and to my great surprise, I found Hemant looking at me from behind the glass doors.

Hemant came out running to meet me. He said that he had left Tulsi to venture into something new. From early 2015, he has become the executive chef and the co-owner of six Indian restaurants in New York City — Chola, Kokam, Chote Nawab, Dhaba, Malai Marke and Haldi. He is now in charge of the kitchen and menus, creating signature dishes and special cuisines inspired by the regional focus of each venue.

Hemant treated us at Haldi and got us an amazing dal prepared at his restaurant, Dhaba. It was a mix of five lentils or what one would commonly refer to as *panchmel dal.* I think my village roots have something to do with my weakness for dal.

I am looking forward to exploring some new places serving Indian food on my ongoing New York trip. Fine dining has surely come of age as far as Indian food in the Big Apple is concerned.

Global Desi's Platter, DNA, Jaipur
November 21, 2015

9

Sampling the NY *Chaat*

My love for Indian food makes me explore all corners of any city I visit. By food, I refer to the desi platter a city has to offer. I love to go to new places serving proper desi cuisine, and also look out for the *chatpata* (mouth-watering) street food that other countries serve. New York scores full marks on both fine dining and street food.

Five Star in Long Island is an Indian eating joint that is operational 24 hours a day. The place reminds me of the famous Azad Hind Dhaba in Kolkata, which the noted painter M.F. Husain loved to frequent.

During my last visit to New York, I had *gol gappas* at this food joint called Kailash Parbat, which is famous for its *chaats.* It has points of presence not only in New York but also in the UK and India, such is their street food branding!

Now onto some news on South Indian food in New York for all foodies. If you happen to go to New York University, you should not miss out on the *dosa-on-thela* on campus.

Tiru Kumar, also known as the 'Dosa-Man Kumar', sells vegan food in front of New York University at Washington Square. "I am a vegan and am proud to sell vegetarian food," he can be heard saying frequently, adding that, "I want Indian food to be tasted internationally."

Kumar hails from Jaffna in Sri Lanka and has a Tamil Nadu connection. For the past 13 years, he has been selling dosa, uttapam and idli. Recently, local authorities allowed him to put his stall inside the university. Before opening this very popular food *thela* (cart) for New York University students, he used to work in a restaurant and, before that, a gas station in 1996. Fascinatingly, for the past 12 years, the prices of his dosa, uttapam, idli and vegetarian roll had remained unchanged. But, of late, his hand has been forced, and prices have been raised after a long spell of surging costs.

Kumar's New York Dosa Tiru Stall has been featured in various food magazines and columns. In Kumar's own words, "I can guarantee you can have dosa if you come at 11am, but if you are late, I can't say you will get one!"

But where there is India, can scams be far behind? Curry House, the Indian restaurant that I had once stopped at for chai, was closed down by the New York Health Department in 2011, citing 67 violations, including adulterated and contaminated food, presence of filth flies, evidence of mice, etc.

Sometime ago, I found myself inside this midtown Manhattan restaurant called Indian Curry House on 160 East, 44 Street, near Grand Central. Enticed by an advertisement for masala chai, I happened to order one. It was absolutely unpalatable, to say the least. Later, I came to know that the Indian place was the same Curry House in its new avatar. It is because of such people that we acquire a tainted identity.

Global Desi's Platter, DNA, Jaipur

December 5, 2015

10

Desi Food in Canada

The strong presence of the Indian diaspora in Canada, where I was last week, has made Indian cuisine popular on this soil, too. Although all big cities in the US, UK and Canada are coming up with new food joints of our desi variety and westerners living there are acquainted with words like 'tandoor', 'tikka', 'paneer', 'naan' etc, it is usually not the case with smaller cities in these countries, where the Indian demographic is far less prominent.

In terms of Indian food abroad, the sad part is that almost anything can be passed off in the name of Indian culture and food these days, even if such items hardly have any Indianness.

In 2011, which was the Year of India in Canada, many artistes and performers came flocking from India. At a show in Quebec, hosted by the Bharati at Place des Arts, the costumes and the faces of the performers were Indian, as was the language of performance, but I could not find anything that was truly Indian in terms of the essence of the music and dance. These kinds of shows have essentially become money-spinning businesses, especially in cities that are a little off-beat and have a lesser Indian population. In another example of the same point, I have even eaten in Bangladeshi restaurants across the world where I have consumed paneer served with pita bread in the name of Indian bread.

Canada, in general, is a country that I love visiting. I have spent quite a few summers in Quebec province in Canada and I love its people and the cold climate.

I was in Ottawa in September. I have been there before too, and although it is the Canadian capital, it has a population of only about a million people — that too with immigrants accounting for seven per cent of the population. After checking in at the Marriott Hotel, I had nothing to do; so, I took Bus No 97 from the Walkley Station close to the hotel to the Rodeo Center, the city's main shopping hub. Whenever I travel to new cities abroad, I always take public transport (if time permits) because that's the best way to explore a new city and observe local peculiarities.

After taking a round of Rodeo Center, I went to the ByWard Market, which is a tourist hub of Ottawa. The area has many eateries and places for a nice outing. I had dinner at an Indian restaurant called Shafali, located in the area. I cannot comment about their non-vegetarian food, but I will definitely not recommend Shafali to Indian vegetarians since there are much better options in the city. The food was very basic, quite like most overseas restaurants, which cater to the westerners' palate.

There was a lone Bengali-speaking girl who was serving there. I also saw a man and a woman in the kitchen, who were talking in Bengali. I guess it was a family-run outlet. In fact, in the bus too, I saw a couple of Bengali students who told me they had recently shifted to Ottawa from Montreal.

The next day, I had a meeting with Katherine, the chairperson of the WFUNA Executive Committee and a few other officials, and after that we went for lunch at an Indian restaurant called East India Company. This restaurant is located at Somerset Street. The food was excellent and the buffet had a lavish spread.

The presence of extreme disparities in the quality of Indian food abroad has, unfortunately, become commonplace in recent decades.

Global Desi's Platter, *DNA*, Jaipur

December 19, 2015

11

The Indian Pulse of Montreal

Rajasthan, Kashmir, Punjab, Jaipur, Ambala, Bombay, Mumbai, Delhi and Mysore... No, I am not recollecting India's geography, but simply referring to the names of the star-rated restaurants in Montreal, located some 12,220 kilometres from my native city of Kolkata. Last month, I flew in from New York to Montreal and checked in at Hotel Hyatt in downtown Montreal.

Francophone Montreal is the largest city in Québec, Canada, with a population around 16 lakhs spread over 19 boroughs. Set on an island on the Saint Lawrence River, it is named after Mount Royal, the tripod-peaked hill at its heart.

The fact that there are over 100 Indian star-rated restaurants dotting the city took me by surprise. Le Taj, Arma, Resto Darbar, Thanjal, Taj Mahal, Thali, Akbar Khana, Bombay Mahal were among some of the popular ones that hotel staff and brochures spoke about. I knew I was spoilt for choice and time being of the essence, I had to choose one.

After a fair amount of back and forth, I settled for Le Taj, given the positive vibes I got about the place from my friends, acquaintances and food critics.

I opted for dinner and lunch at Le Taj, which is famous for its Indian food not just in Montreal but in the entirety of North America. Located in downtown Montreal, Le Taj has built its reputation over the past three decades as an eatery of excellence. The restaurant's specially trained staff treat every guest like a celebrity.

The restaurant's visible *tandoor* (clay oven) gives the visitors a view of the chefs at work preparing gastronomic delights like lamb chops, kebabs, garlic shrimps, chicken tikka and an assortment of naans. The lunch buffet is inexpensive, with a symphony of vegetarian and non-vegetarian dishes. The food is popular and the chefs keep busy throughout the week.

I met the owner, Vinod Kapoor, who left his native village in the beautiful Mussoorie hills in 1985 to follow his heart's calling to set up a restaurant. Vinod told me that they were celebrating 30 years of the restaurant, for which they had put up a stack of memorabilia — mostly pictures of celebrities and important events that happened there during the past three decades.

The interiors, too, speak of the restaurant's Indian connection. A mud wall adorns the rear section of Le Taj. This wall was part of the Indian Pavilion at Expo 67, held in Montreal.

Inside the restaurant, I had a pleasant feeling of being inside a museum of sorts. There are several intriguing items of Indian and Tibetan art and crafts on display. Three intricately fashioned panels, once a part of Expo 67, are positioned at the entrance. Also, a huge mural, saved by Kapoor from the Expo, amplifies the restaurant's elegant ambience along with plaster carvings and terracotta-coloured walls. It is Indian without necessarily being ethnic.

Culinary attractions are aplenty in Montreal and I think it is a dream city for any Indian foodie who wants to explore. Besides Le Taj, I came to know about the Jai Ho Thali at Akbar Khana restaurant. If in the mood for South Indian food, I was told there is Thurpal. Maybe next time.

Food Wise, DNA, Jaipur

January 2, 2016

12

When *Firangi* Food Was the Flavour of Pink City

With so many foreigners descending on the recently concluded Jaipur Literature Festival (JLF) — what with January being the peak tourist season as well — *firangi* (foreign) food was in great demand. After all, not every foreigner is a fan of spicy Indian curries!

While the JLF lunch on all the five days had yummy pasta served with both red and white sauces, there was also an ample serving of air-fried vegetables to go with the pasta. These edibles were in great demand both among the foreign as well as Indian delegates. Not to forget that Jacob's Creek wine — both red and white — paired very well with the pasta and vegetables.

Those who did not have pasta had the no less-enviable choice of having some excellent thin-crust margherita pizzas and stuffed tomatoes with focaccia bread at the Home Café stall. They gelled well with coffee —

Cappuccino, Americana and Latte. At the nearby Punjab Grill eatery, some enterprising folks also brought some excellent Sangria to go with their Italian food.

Throughout the event, the foreign visitors as well as Indians loving western food had the choice to go to Anokhi Café, On the House, Home Café or Taru Veda.

Anokhi Café, for instance, is known to serve some of the best lemon meringue tarts, bagels and cream cheese, falafel, corn fritters, Thai bean salad, feta tapenade and blue cheese salad. The best part about Anokhi's cuisines is that the organic vegetables served here are grown on the Anokhi farm in Jaipur.

The English breakfast at On the House is also quite popular, comprising bacon rashes, chicken sausages, fried tomatoes, baked beans and hash browns, not to forget an eclectic spread of eggs — ranging from Mediterranean omelettes to Egg Florentine. Yet another recommendation from the eatery would be the burrito — the choice being among vegetables, chicken and lamb.

If you are in the mood for all things British, then nothing beats the fish and chips of Home Café. Also, one can go in for a classic British delicacy of salmon, cream cheese and shallots. The restaurant strongly recommends the bread and butter pudding of eggs, cheddar cheese and, of course, bread.

Taru Veda has a classic Canadian dish called Poutine, served with crispy wedges, cheese curds and a mushroom gravy. The visitors here also love poached eggs in Italian sauce with beans and feta. Sushi (both veg and non-veg) is in great demand here and is served with wasabi cream, Japanese ginger and soy sauce.

The best part about these eateries is that the food does not burn a big hole in your pocket. In terms of cleanliness, service, ambience and, of course, the all-important deliciousness quotient, I would heartily recommend all these terrific outlets at JLF.

Food Wise, DNA, Jaipur
February 6, 2016

13

Indian *Tadka* in Bangkok

Recently, I was visiting Southeast Asian countries and happened to be in Thailand, which is a favourite Indian as well as global tourist destination. There is a one-lakh strong Indian diaspora and it is quite common to find Indian restaurants in every nook and corner of not only Bangkok but also the other cities of Pattaya, Phuket, Chiang Mai and so on. A few Bangladeshi restaurants, with cuisines similar to India's, can also be found.

Thai cuisine is unique and has its own identity like its French, Italian or Mediterranean counterparts. Among Asian countries, Thailand is considered to have been influenced by Indian and Chinese traditions. Yet, those who experience it find it very different from Indian, Chinese or Japanese cuisines and say it is easily identifiable in its own right. There is a reason for this.

Thailand was the only Southeast Asian country never to be colonised by the West. The Thai people migrated to their present homeland from the Wuhan province of

China some 2,000 years ago. They also brought their spicy cooking style and dietary staple — rice. Thailand has developed an advanced culinary tradition of fine dining that even rivals Indian cuisine in its reputation of being spicy. The use of aquatic animals, herbs and plants is very common. Thai street food, too, is immensely popular with tourists.

The characteristics of Thai cuisine depend on who cooks, for whom and where (which part of Thailand). Skewing, baking and grilling are very common. Like ghee (clarified butter) in India, Thai cooking uses a lot of coconut milk and dairy products. A vast variety of local vegetables are the natural taste enhancers.

Being a global tourist destination, many foreign visitors have had an opportunity to taste and like Thai food. Many have gone back to their countries and set up Thai food restaurants thereafter. Then there are others like chef Gaggan Anand, who went to Thailand from India in 2007 and set up an Indian restaurant (named after himself) in Bangkok in 2010, currently located in the city's sub-district of Lumphini.

Although I have been to Thailand many times, I have never tasted the local food. Thai cuisine, being predominantly non-vegetarian, is said to be unique, with its subtle balance of aromatic components and spices. Although I do not have any experience of having Thai food, I think a vegetarian like myself cannot go very far with the cuisine.

Kolkata-born Gaggan calls his style 'progressive Indian House cuisine', which is a euphemism for fusion food. Gaggan, a former drummer who received a diploma in catering from Thiruvananthapuram, worked for many restaurants during his early days in Bangkok. The concept of starting the progressive Indian food joint was a result of his frustration during training, when his desire to do something different clashed with the conventional training approach and method.

Earlier, most Indian restaurants in Thailand used to offer South Indian as well as North Indian food. But recently, the concept of Indian fusion food in Thailand has taken off. *TIME* magazine has dubbed Gaggan Anand the 'Captain Kirk of cuisine' and his restaurant is rated among the top 50 Asian restaurants.

Gaggan's eponymous restaurant has limited seats and frequently receives calls for advanced booking. Some of his delicacies, in terms of presentation, have risen to an art form. Even I had the pleasure of experiencing one of the dishes, which looked like a lump of burnt-out charcoal, but when on my palate, tasted heavenly.

Food Wise, *DNA*, Jaipur

April 9, 2016

14

Taste of Home at Bangkok's Rang Mahal

I am in Bangkok where the rains have started. When I think of a desi food outlet, the first thing that comes to my mind is the Indian restaurant Rang Mahal in Hotel Rembrandt, located in the Sukhumvit area of central Bangkok.

Hotel Rembrandt was my address in Bangkok in 1994-95 when I first landed in Thailand and continued to be so till 2004 because it housed, among other restaurants, Rang Mahal.

My first trip to Thailand was unplanned and unscheduled. I was in England when there was an outbreak of plague in India and all major flights were stopped. I was supposed to return home via Moscow. But there weren't any options. The only favour the airlines did was to reroute my flight to Kolkata via Bangkok instead of Moscow.

I had no hotel booking or any contact at that time in Bangkok. At the airport I asked the hotel counter to book me a hotel where I could get some Indian food, for I was sick of eating French fries. That's how I reached Bangkok and ended up in Hotel Rembrandt and came to know about Rang Mahal.

Hotel Rembrandt has many foreign restaurants — Red Pepper (Thai), Mexicano, Italian restaurant Da Vinci, and Flavours (multicuisine) and, of course, my favourite Indian restaurant, Rang Mahal, which is located on the hotel's rooftop on the 26th floor with a 360-degree view of the city.

With chandeliers, candles and live music, the restaurant has a regal ambience. I have been to Rang Mahal many times and I think it is one of the top Indian restaurants in Bangkok specialising in North Indian cuisine. For the past two decades, Rang Mahal has been winning the best Indian restaurant award. The restaurant also has a live Indian music band that performs old hits of Mukesh and Rafi.

Among those who manage Rang Mahal are head chef Rajan Misra and manager Varun. The manager is always close by to help you choose from a lavish spread that covers exotic fine dining cuisines to Indian street food like *aloo tikki* with tamarind and mint sauce.

For vegetarians, Mixed Vegetable Takatak is a colourful mix of seasonal vegetables served on a *tawa* (cast iron griddle). Also, the mildly spiced green peas dish is excellent. Masala onions and masala papad are a real treat that keep the Indian spirits high.

Rang Mahal continues to improvise and respond to various occasions, like the Satvik Navratri Vrat Thali was introduced during the Navratri celebrations. Rang Mahal's Sunday brunch is also much sought-after. The regular thalis, too, are immensely popular and I have lost count as to how many such thalis I have ordered for myself and my guests till date.

The restaurant has an amazing view of the city and even today, the last corner table near the full glass panel is my favourite spot, though it is hard to get unless booked in advance. For regulars like myself, however, there is always an exception!

Food Wise, DNA, Jaipur

May 21, 2016

15

Maya Casts its *Jaal* in Bangkok

Last week I was in Thailand again and visited Bawarchi restaurant. It was Visakha Bucha Day — a national holiday in Thailand. Visakha Bucha Day is the most auspicious of the Thai Buddhist holidays as it commemorates three important anniversaries in the life of Lord Buddha — his birth, his enlightenment and his passing away.

I went to the Bawarchi restaurant branch located at the President Tower Arcade (Intercontinental Bangkok). I have always admired this restaurant and every time I am in Bangkok, I order food from Bawarchi on a daily basis, having it delivered to the Grand Hyatt Hotel.

In fact, more than by sight, the restaurant staff recognise me by name. I have had the pleasure of meeting Vinay Chawla, an extremely humble gentleman, who is the vice-president of this chain of restaurants. Apart from this one, there are three more Bawarchi restaurants around the world, including one in Myanmar and one in Gurgaon.

I also met Arijit Ghosh, who was a chef at the Taj Jai Mahal Palace in Jaipur and now takes care of Bawarchi. Arijit wishes to open his own restaurant, and seeing his abilities, I am sure he will not only succeed but also make it big. I wish him all the best.

Although Bangkok is full of Indian restaurants, Thailand's other cities don't have good quality Indian food to offer except for the Indian wedding caterers.

Before I end my desi food journal in Thailand, there is another restaurant I would like to mention and that is Maya. It is located in the Sukhumvit area on the 29th floor of Hotel Holiday Inn, Bangkok.

I really liked Maya on my first visit. While entering, it somehow gives you the feeling of Rang Mahal as this is also housed on the top floor of a hotel, overlooking the city. Maya has a posh lounge area, a bar, a separate dining area and a variety of Indian fusion food menus. Though they don't have any *chaat* or kebab festivals, they do have attractions like Music Night on Fridays, Ladies' Night on Wednesdays and so on.

The open kitchen gives you an inside view of the large copper tandoor ovens and as you stare out of the large glass panels, there is a grand view of the Bangkok cityscape.

Traditional food in its modern avatar, friendly staff and great taste define Maya. Chef Ramnik Singh Lamba supervises the delicious North Indian dishes. Some of the dishes, like Dal Maya with naan, I am told, are very popular. The restaurant also has a Bar Snacks wing, where you can find exotic cocktails mixed with beetroot, cinnamon, cumin powder, pudina, guava juice, sugarcane juice, mint and so on.

If you are an Indian foodie in Bangkok, just like Gaggan and Rang Mahal, you should not miss out on Maya, either. However, if you want to have your food while perched on your couch in the hotel, then Bawarchi is still the best option.

Global Desi's Platter, DNA, Jaipur

June 4, 2016

16

The Essence of Indian Food in Singapore

I remember it was on the eve of May Day last year that I landed in Singapore. Most of the shops were closed that day. I headed towards Clarke Quay or CQ, as it is commonly known, to savour a dining experience at the RAS. Clarke Quay is a historical riverside quay in Singapore and is famous for its nightlife, wining and dining.

RAS, the Indian food joint, is located at CQ Square, just before the river bridge crossing. It is open from seven in the morning till late at night and the last order has to be placed by 11.30pm.

I reached there in the nick of time, just before the counters stopped working. Singapore, being a stickler for rules, would not have bent them had I been late even by a nano second.

RAS claims to showcase the essence of India with contemporary Indian dining as its forte. The Indian food that it serves is more than just Rajasthani dal or Kashmiri naan — from what the restaurant tells its customers. People naturally visit with a lot of expectations. Along with the 'vibrant' and 'palate-soothing' delicacies, they also serve fine wines.

I, too, visited with a lot of expectations, having read about the place. However, I was a little disappointed. I found the restaurant very basic and although they keep harping about 'unsurpassed service', I felt the service was not up to the mark and the staff was lacking in hospitality.

While the food was okay, what surprised me more was the fact that this restaurant, located in one of the most happening and expensive areas of Singapore, manages to carry on with its less-than-average service. Probably, being the only Indian restaurant in this prime location has helped it prosper, and to foreigners, the Indian food they serve seems nice. I am not aware if any other Indian restaurant has come up in the area afterwards.

I shared my experience with a few others and most agreed that being an expensive restaurant, its service could have been better.

When I talk of Indian food in Singapore, the name Woodlands comes back to me with a lot of nostalgia. I had wonderful, out-of-the-world South Indian food at this place 15 years ago when I had first visited the city-state. I later heard that it had also started serving North Indian dishes.

However, during my visit to Singapore three years ago, I found out upon enquiry that the place had closed down. The new labour laws in the country had a lot to do with its closure, as overseas employment became difficult. This is really sad as I can still recall the taste of spongy idlis and paper-thin dosas that kept a vegetarian like me going for many days. One can still find Woodlands in Singapore upon searching online, but I am not sure if it's the same or a different place altogether. I need to find this out on my next visit to Singapore.

Global Desi's Platter, *DNA*, Jaipur
June 18, 2016

17

Memories of Punjab in Singapore

In recent times, a restaurant that has become a must-visit in Singapore is the Punjab Grill at Marina Bay Sands, belonging to the celebrated chef, Jiggs Kalra. He is constantly referred to as the 'Czar of Indian cuisine' and the first Asian to be inducted into the International Gourmet Hall of Fame.

In their own words, 'to dine at Punjab Grill is to take an epicurean journey through India's richly diverse gourmet metropolises.'

Punjab Grill draws its inspiration from the regal grandeur of the Maharajas. Done in glass and metal, the entrance to the restaurant is sure to dazzle one's eyes. As I enter, the light reflecting in the glass interiors blinds me for a moment, with the shiny copper vessels used for tandoor adding to the splendour.

As the name suggests, the Punjab Grill cuisine is from

the North West Frontier Province, a part of the erstwhile undivided Punjab. This includes gourmet dishes from Lahore, Multan, Rawalpindi, Peshawar, Amritsar and Kabul. The moment 'Punjabi cuisine' is mentioned, the image of *makki ki roti* and *sarson da saag* is sure to come to your mind but Punjab Grill shows people that there is so much more to Punjabi food.

At this restaurant, the food and the service were far better than my expectations and the menu, too, had a lot of variety. Let me share with you the kind of food you will get at Singapore's Punjab Grill. For weekdays, they have set menus that they call Weekday Power Lunch. For leisurely weekends, they have the elaborate kebab and biryani feast. There is yet another menu called Executive Set Lunch. All the menus cater to both vegetarians and non-vegetarians. There is also the à la carte menu.

The credit goes to Punjab Grill for reinventing old recipes that were once secretly guarded by the royal cooks, besides creating some innovative ones that have now become signature dishes. These are Dahi ke Kebab, Kurkure, Salmon Tikka and Paan Shot, among several others. Some names are also attached to the dishes to give an idea of the region it originates from — Paneer Tikka Multani, Lahori Seekh, Pindi Chana and Patiala Shahi Machchhi.

Being a vegetarian, I often have difficulty in choosing dishes in restaurants but this place was considerate enough to have a very good vegetarian platter, too. What I relished here the most was Tarkari Kesari Biryani, Amritsari Malai Kofta, Dal Punjab Grill, Hara Bhara Kabab and Patiala Shahi Kadai Paneer.

Before my meal, I opted to have a *Mattha* as an aperitif. What caught my eye were some names that could transport you to the actual places, like Chowk Ki Tikki. Although I was tempted to have the Kesar Pista Wali Lassi, I stayed away for fear of adding more calories.

It is not for nothing that Punjab Grill has won so many awards. It is rated among the top 10 restaurants in Singapore. Recognised as a premier fine dining restaurant, it has been gathering accolades continuously. Their chef, Javed Ahamad, has also bagged the title of Asian Cuisine Chef of the Year from World Gourmet Summit.

So, when in Singapore and looking for some excellent Indian cuisine, waste no time — you know where to go.

Food Wise, DNA, Jaipur

July 2, 2016

18

Rasam, *Shorba* and More in Malaysia

London becomes the address of who's who in the summers — the Taj Group-owned St. James' Court Hotel and apartments being a favourite of many. I met a Malaysia-based Indian family by chance at Hampton Bar while having my *dal chawal* and the discussion headed to desi food in Malaysia. In the meantime, news had arrived of David Cameron ordering Indian cuisine for his last dinner as Prime Minister.

I first visited Malaysia about six years ago. Though I have had the Malaysian visa for quite some time, I was not able to go because of one reason or the other. When I finally reached the country, it was just before our Independence Day and I attended the celebrations at the Indian High Commission. During my visit, I was informed by the then Indian High Commissioner, Sri Vijay K. Gokhale, that Malaysia had the highest number of Persons of Indian

Origin (PIOs) — almost 20 million at that time. Indians were everywhere and it felt as if I was in India itself.

There were lots of eateries of all kinds. Because of the multicultural environment in Malaysia that includes Chinese, Indian Muslims and Tamilians from both India and Sri Lanka, apart from the Malays, food is bound to be diverse. Talking about Indian food, there are many restaurants serving North Indian, but even more for South Indian food.

My first tryst with local food was when I visited Bi-Jan restaurant, which claims to serve traditional Malay cuisine. The warm and serene interiors create an ambience that reflects the spirit of modern Malaysia. The menu features many traditional Malay dishes — from popular ones to rare and forgotten recipes from the villages locally known as 'kampung' food. After returning late at night, I pleasantly discovered a 24x7 dosa shop near Hotel Lotus. Thanks to that, I did not have to sleep on an empty stomach as my vegetarian habits had prevented me from eating at Bi-Jan earlier.

Intent on trying out the vegetarian food on offer, I later went to the Spice of India restaurant. The restaurant is located at a shopping mall underneath the twin Petronas Towers. The place welcomes you with large mirrors and lush silk drapes and specialises in both North and South

Indian dishes. Hence, there are *rasams* along with *shorbas* on the menu. The ample variety comprises samosas, pakoras, tikkas, *kulchas*, seekh kebabs (I mean the vegetarian kind), rotis, naans and parathas. For a vegetarian like me, it was an ideal situation in a foreign land. I particularly fancied the *makhani paratha* and cheese naan stuffed with dry fruits and nuts.

I was pleasantly surprised to see the varieties of rice on the menu. There was *nimbu chawal,* tamarind rice, *zafrani chawal, zeera chawal* and *matar pulao* apart from biryani. Lassis also came in various types, not just sweet or salt but Rose Lassi, Mango Lassi and Pudina Lassi, too. The only thing that I found expensive compared to the others was the masala chai, whereas the other kinds of tea like Earl Grey, Darjeeling and Iced Tea cost much less. The food tasted fine and I had nothing much to complain about on foreign soil.

Global Desi's Platter, DNA, Jaipur

July 16, 2016

19

Rajesh Khanna Cooks in Malaysia!

During my first visit to Malaysia in 2010, I stayed at the Sheraton Imperial, Kuala Lumpur, which is located in the heart of the city's commercial and business district. From my room on the 37th floor, I could clearly see the twin Petronas Towers, standing at an astonishing 1,483 feet. The towers were made famous by the Hollywood film, *Entrapment,* featuring Sean Connery and Catherine Zeta-Jones, as many of you will remember.

Sheraton Imperial Kuala Lumpur is a five-star luxury property mainly designed for holding business conventions and conferences. But I felt that the hotel needed significant improvement considering it was a premium range hotel.

As I checked in around midnight, I wanted to have some food — vegetarian, of course. I was appalled when the hotel's kitchen could not provide me with even a basic tomato soup!

I was all the more surprised when I was told later that the hotel had an Indian-origin chef and the executive chef, too, was an Indian with wide knowledge and skills to rustle up all types of Indian dishes. The interesting part was that the chef was named Rajesh Khanna, after the Bollywood superstar. The chef's father was a great fan of the actor and named his son after him.

After meeting and requesting chef Rajesh, he cooked for me some excellent Indian vegetarian dishes. Considering that he had never been to India, his knowledge of desi Indian food was quite impressive. What a relief it was to find him, as I was at my wits' end not knowing what to do, having not even found a soup earlier.

The Italian restaurant of the hotel — Villa Danieli — was styled like a country home offering homely food and the best of wines. The 421-metre high Kuala Lumpur Tower could be seen from there, along with its revolving restaurant. Although smaller in height compared to the Petronas Towers, one still cannot overlook the sheer majesty of KL Tower. The revolving restaurant is called Seri Angkasa, where I had lunch with some UN officials discussing the possibility of the United Nations and its associations working more closely.

Seri Angkasa is now called Atmosphere 360, and rightly so, as it actually gives you a 360-degree panoramic view of the city. There was a huge spread of salads and some vegetarian dishes, too. Plus, the usual local fare like *rendang* and a seafood spread, apart from desserts and fresh fruits.

The buffet section offered a selection of local, Chinese, Indian and Western food. I found some unusual flavours of ice creams, like sweet corn and sweet potato. The food at this revolving restaurant wasn't that great but the view of the city was breathtaking and made the visit a memorable one. An important tip for those who would like to have a window seat for the 360-degree view — you need to book your seat well in advance. The rates are reasonable and if one does not fuss about food too much, I would recommend the place as the view is unmatched and definitely compensates for all the gastronomic shortcomings.

Having said that, for all the joy of mesmerising views, nothing beats chef Rajesh's desi food!

Global Desi's Platter, DNA, Jaipur

July 30, 2016

20

A First for the Olympics: Indian Food

The Rio Olympics has got sports lovers all around the world incredibly excited, as they keenly await new superstars to emerge and past records to be broken. It is not possible to talk of new world records at the Games just yet. However, there are definitely some 'firsts' as far as India is concerned.

The most interesting thing that has happened to the Indian contingent this year is the availability of Indian food. The Sports Ministry has made it possible for Indian athletes to have Indian food at the Olympic village. Prime Minister Narendra Modi has been instrumental in the implementation of this move. For the first time, athletes will be able to have *dal chawal* so that they do not miss home and, perhaps more importantly for some, can perform better. I have also heard that the ITC group of hotels sent two chefs to Rio to cater to the needs of desi food among the athletes.

About six months ago, the Olympic Committee had rejected this proposal for Indian food saying it would not be possible to include an Indian kitchen as the Indian contingent was too small. But the ministry pursued the matter saying that this time the Indian contingent was bigger than previous occasions and that this food could also be eaten by members of other South Asian countries like Bangladesh and Sri Lanka. The dishes include dal makhani, vegetable pulao, raita, sambar, tandoori chicken, egg *bhurji* and gulab jamun.

Food is an important issue at such an event as several participants, being vegetarians, prefer vegetarian meals, and in international events, adequate vegetarian options are often unavailable for these players. With the additional restriction on players to eat only in the Olympic Village, food and nutrition often becomes a major hurdle.

As finding a chef for the Indian section in Brazil was difficult, a chef from India was flown to Rio to look after the Asian section. Ishan Bahukhandi from Uttarakhand is a Delhi-based chef who is excited at his new assignment and is said to have taken with him a lot of spices from India.

The news makes me particularly happy, leading me to recount my culinary experiences in Brazil. When I went to Rio about four years ago, I had discovered that there were about 350 Indian families in Brazil, of which 20 to 25 lived in Rio, but there were no Indian restaurants there. It was strange that in a city of 13 million population, there was no Indian food joint despite the global popularity of tandoori dishes.

A Google search showed a couple of places as Indian restaurants, but these were not good enough, and hence closed down soon. In fact, there is not a single shop where you can get Indian groceries. As a result, Indians living in Rio carry their foodstuff like pulses from India or from other cities of Brazil.

So great is the lure of Indian food that I know of a cricketer, Vimarshan, playing for a Brazilian state and stationed in Rio, who takes a two-hour flight to go to Curitiba (in the state of Paraná) simply to have Indian food.

I sincerely wish all the best to all our players in Rio; I am sure they will perform excellently as their food intake will not be an issue this time. Thank you very much, Mr Prime Minister.

Global Desi's Platter, DNA, Jaipur

August 13, 2016

21

Wafting Indian Aromas in Brazil

During my stay in Rio, I gathered that most Indians in Brazil live in São Paulo. Though quite a few of them are also spread across Rio, Brasilia, Manaus, São José dos Campos and Curitiba.

With the exception of São Paulo and Curitiba, getting Indian food is like a dream come true for Indians in Brazil. But Brazil is one country that allows 32 kilos in two pieces of baggage if one travels by air in any class. Thus, it enables many Indians to get their favourite foods from India. As pulses are not available and there are no grocery shops selling any Indian food stuff, the rule regarding this allowance naturally makes Indians very happy.

In early 2000, I remember dining with Lakhi Daswani, the owner of the Indian restaurant, Tandoor, in São Paulo. He told me that he had procured every Indian ingredient from his daughter, who was living in the US. Daswani was a very prominent Indian settled in Brazil and his Tandoor was said to be the best Indian outlet not only in Brazil but in all of Latin America. Today there are about 20 Indian restaurants in São Paulo.

Recently, Lakhi Daswani was in Kolkata, visiting India after decades. I spent an evening with him and his family and, of course, discussed desi food available in Latin America.

The popularity and pull of Indian food are such that even in Brazil Indians travel across cities just to get a taste of home. I had earlier mentioned Vimarshan, who played cricket for the state team in Brazil and lived in Rio but often took a two-hour flight to Curitiba to eat at Swadisht, an Indian restaurant run by the Keshwani family.

Coming back to Indian food in São Paulo, I must talk a little more of Tandoor. I was pleasantly surprised that this was one of the very few places which actually had very good vegetarian options. Usually with my vegetarian taste buds I find it a little difficult to find authentic Indian food abroad. Even in so-called Indian food joints, I find a limited choice of vegetarian food and even where I find it, the taste, in most of the cases, is not up to the mark.

Tandoor is evidently the first choice for both vegetarians and non-vegetarians for its vast array of foods on the menu. I must talk of the different kinds of rotis and breads available — plain or butter naan, cheese naan, garlic naan, *pudina kulcha, aloo kulcha, pyaz kulcha,* tandoori roti, *roomali* roti, chapati and paratha.

The vegetable menu offers a cross-section of dishes such as Aloo Kashmiri and Vegetable Kolhapuri. There are several paneer dishes and other delicious fare, including *baingan bharta, chana masala, malai kofta* and *khumb malai.* In the *sobremesa* or dessert section there are kulfis, gulab jamuns and ice cream. Although I do not have much of a sweet tooth, I loved the gulab jamun, which also happens to be the most popular dessert in the restaurant. Apart from lassi, the other non-alcoholic drink that caught my attention was sherbet made with rose essence.

I was drawn towards the vegetarian thali on the menu and I felt happy that this was available in a foreign country. Before departing, I thanked Lakhi for solving the problem of vegetarians in an alien land where explaining the concept of vegetarian food can be a challenge in itself.

Global Desi's Platter, DNA, Jaipur

August 27, 2016

22

Rajasthani Meets Italian

I did a little bit of research before going to Rome last week to witness the historic moment of Mother Teresa's canonisation at the Vatican. My research was confined to food as I was planning to host a dinner for my acquaintances. I did not have to try too hard as I came to know from some diplomat friends that an Indian restaurant called Jaipur was right there in the centre of Trastevere.

I was even more excited because of its name and my own association with the Pink City. Ristorante Indiano Jaipur — this is what is written on its doorway. What I also noticed was a lemon and a few chilies hanging at the entrance — so typically Indian — to ward off the evil eye or *buri nazar.*

As one enters the restaurant, it feels as if you are in India itself. The décor, complete with Rajasthani paintings and brass statues, is quintessentially Indian. The owner, Pradeep Kumar, who has been in Italy for over 30 years, was involved in constructional engineering and later switched to the restaurant business. Pradeep has his roots in Rajasthan's Chirana. He is now helped by his brother-in-law, Mahendra Singh Chauhan, who hails from Jaipur. Pradeep opened Jaipur in 2001 and Mahendra joined his *jijaji* (sister's husband) the following year. As his family still lives in Jaipur, Mahendra comes here thrice a year. His brother Sunny, who has also joined the business, was my one-point contact.

I must admit I was so touched by Pradeep and Mahendra's warmth and simplicity that I have no words to thank them. They were so well-mannered and cultured that it was impossible not to be impressed. Some of their customers, too, talk of the warmth and hospitality they exude from within.

The restaurant claims to be a tandoor specialist. The menu, although in Italian, has options like Humari Rasoi Se, featuring samosas, *bondas*, pakoras etc.

Tandoori Khana lists a series of items — both veg and non-veg, made with oriental herbs. The menu card lists an array of non-vegetarian items but I stopped at Verdure e Legumi. From *saag aloo, aloo matar, malai kofta, kumbi* and *gobhi masala* cooked in Rajasthani style to varieties of dal, there is no shortage of vegetarian options.

Then, of course, are the usual rice dishes like pulao and biryani. There are naans, kulchas and parathas, too.

Although not too fond of sweets, I couldn't help gazing at the dessert fare — *rasmalai,* kulfi (their specialty) made of mango and coconut, gulab jamun and *gajar ka halwa* are the regular fixtures.

It was very strange to see that there were Indian wines and beers available, given that in India we look for Italian wines!

Additionally, if they know you are from Rajasthan, they give you dry paan as well.

My dinner party was held in the hall at the back of the restaurant. Both in terms of food and service, I had nothing to complain about. In fact, I have to say that this is the best I have ever got anywhere.

Not for nothing do the diners come up with remarks like 'the best Indian restaurant in Rome', 'a homely place' and 'exquisite food'. I also learnt that the Indian Mission in Rome hosts parties here. I now know why people even in Kolkata mentioned the name Jaipur instantly when I sought suggestions for my dinner venue.

Thank you, Pradeep and Mahendra, for setting up Jaipur and giving people the opportunity to know all about Indian food and hospitality in Rome.

Global Desi's Platter, DNA, Jaipur

September 10, 2016

23

Starving in Incheon

I had first visited South Korea as a judge for the Asia-Pacific Model UN. We were in Incheon, located in north-western South Korea. Back then, Incheon had just started being promoted by South Korea to become a conference city like Geneva.

Today, Incheon is an international city popular for conferences and the Incheon airport is considered to be one of the largest and broadest in the world. The Asian Games were held at Incheon in 2014. It has been rated as the best airport since 2005. The city has a population of three million.

But that visit of mine to Korea has left an indelible mark on my memory. I still wonder how I survived. I have read that it is one of the worst countries as far as vegetarian food is concerned. Even then, what I suffered there is nothing short of a nightmare.

Here was a modern, clean city with a top-notch hotel, but when it came to food, specifically vegetarian food, the result was a huge disappointment. When I faced problems finding food, I Googled and found an Indian restaurant but, that too, to my dismay, was shut down. In the end I had to ask Hotel Radisson for a microwave so that I could boil some vegetables to eat. On the entire trip, I had to survive on Korean rice and tomato puree alone.

Even the airport that looked so clean and beautiful couldn't offer me any food that I could consume. I wondered how it would be possible to promote the place as a conference city at par with Geneva if there was no attempt or focus on the availability of food — keeping in mind the multicultural tastes of people.

In all my travels across the globe, I have faced many situations where I had limited choice in terms of food. In my book of travels — *Aap Biti Jag Biti* — I have mentioned Peru's Machu Picchu, where I had to eat sandwiches by removing the fish from the filling — that was the awareness level as far as vegetarianism was concerned. But even then, my Incheon food experience cannot be compared to anywhere else at all.

I was practically starving. South Korea is one of the highest meat-consuming countries in the world, but I had failed to understand that it would be the reason for next-to-nil vegetarian options. My hosts were at their wits' end about what to feed me. Leave alone Indian food, there was absolutely no vegetarian food available anywhere in the entire city of Incheon!

Today, when I Google names of Indian restaurants in the city, quite a few crop up. Jyoti seems to be the most popular restaurant, followed by Taj, Ganga, Namaste, Asia, Swagat and several others. At present, vegetarian food is also available, as reflected in the restaurant reviews.

My Incheon food experience has made me realise how important a role food plays in a person's life. One can survive and fight against all odds but when it comes to food, there is no middle path — you either eat or you don't.

With my near-starvation experience, I know what one's plight is when one visits a country for work. Food need not be fanciful and attractive to your eyes but it is important to make available basic and palatable food — only to survive.

Today when we talk of the world as a global village, the basic option of having adequate varieties of food becomes a prerequisite for any place to gain an international status. Thankfully, today's Incheon is a far cry from the Incheon I had known.

Global Desi's Platter, DNA, Jaipur
September 24, 2016

24

Korea — Eating Like the Indians Do!

Food always makes travel interesting — I say interesting as it may not always turn out to be a pleasant affair. If your taste buds do not respond favourably to the food you are tasting, it would be regarded as an unpleasant experience. In the last column I had mentioned my food experience in Incheon, where eating anything was an issue. Being a vegetarian, I cannot be too experimental with food during my travels abroad.

One can find plenty of good Indian restaurants in countries like Malaysia and Singapore as there is a sizable Indian community living there. But I was surprised to see that even in a country like South Korea, there are many good Indian restaurants, most of which have come up recently. I have been to Seoul more than once and every time I see the city, I feel amazed at the cleanliness, the discipline and the fast pace of the country. But at the same time, the people are very warm and friendly.

According to the latest reports, there are more than 7,000 Indians living in Seoul. These include scholars, scientists and software professionals. I was told that there are several Indians apart from those staying illegally in the country.

Indian food seems to be very popular in the country as there are several Indian joints run by Indians, Pakistanis and Nepalis. To give you an idea of their popularity, I am listing some of the better-known names: Everest, Jyoti, Taj Palace, Bombay Grill, Saffron, Namaste, Chakra, Shanti, Utsav, Amma and many more. Then there is Agra, Benaras, Yamuna and Ganga too — all unmistakably Indian in their names.

There is a strange-sounding restaurant called Pocala, which serves Tibetan food along with Indian cuisine. The best thing about this place is that if they have a vegetarian customer, they serve food especially prepared for them — without even onion and garlic — that is, Jain food. It is because of this that they get a lot of vegetarian customers. Yamuna also serves vegetarian food (Jain food), cooked in separate utensils to maintain the highest hygiene standards. It is actually very strange to find Indian restaurants in Seoul serving customised food for Jains on the one hand, and on the other, seeing restaurants with names like Durga, Om or Ganga serving non-vegetarian food.

Some time ago, I had read a comparative study on India and Korea in an international magazine, hinting at the fact that although both countries had similar backgrounds and problems, South Korea had raced past India and is today a developed country while India is still developing. It is a depressing thought indeed. But what makes me feel better is the popularity of Indian cuisine in the country — way ahead of what Korean food enjoys in India.

An indicator of the popularity of Indian cuisine is the fact that several South Korean restaurants also have branches. For example, Otsal is a popular Indian restaurant near Seoul National University. This was founded in 1998 and has many branches. Namaste is another chain of Indian restaurants authentically decorated with Indian artefacts and serving, apart from classic Indian cuisines, food like samosas, pakoras and their specialty — chai.

I have not been to too many places in Seoul that serve Indian food. But the interesting news is that in the heart of Seoul, one can taste *prasadam* in the only Krishna temple located here. Although I have not had the opportunity myself, I have heard from others that it is probably the best vegetarian food available in the city.

Global Desi's Platter, DNA, Jaipur

October 8, 2016

25

The Seoul Experience

I came to Seoul from Incheon after a Model UN and checked into The Plaza. It is an old hotel but newly done up and has good modern facilities. But the best thing about the place is its fantastic location — near the City Hall and the royal palace. It is also close to the two UNESCO sites — Jongmyo and Changdeokgung.

As I wrote earlier about my time with regard to food in Incheon, I decided to comment on the food in Seoul this time around. I found several restaurants where Indian food was available. I set out of my hotel and after a few queries, came to a place called Ganga. I looked at the woman with folded hands on the billboard claiming to serve authentic Indian cuisine. It reassured me that I would be able to find the kind of food I wanted. It was lunch time and Ganga was completely packed. I was bent upon eating at this place so I wanted to book a table for the evening. They said no table was available. But I insisted and requested, as I was desperate — what with my near-starving experience at Incheon.

At last, they gave in and gave me a reservation for just 30 minutes from the time the restaurant was to open in the evening. I was elated and thanked them profusely.

Ganga is situated at the Seoul Finance Centre. The travel time from my hotel was just five minutes. An expensive restaurant, no doubt, but from the ambience and the crowd, it was evident that this was a popular place. The fact that Indian cuisine is popular here is reinforced by the fact that Ganga has over nine branches in South Korea.

The feedback that I gathered was quite mixed, as some felt the food was not authentic. However, it sounded strange as I heard the chef was from India, with over 20 years of experience. Tandoor items seemed to be a rage. I got to know that the most popular items at Ganga are naan, tandoori chicken, samosas and gulab jamuns.

I tasted Dal Bukhara, Palak Paneer and naan as, being a vegetarian, I had limited options. Of course, there were some other options like Paneer Butter Masala or Paneer Makhani and vegetable dishes like Malai Kofta, Aloo Gobhi and Vegetable Bhurji. I did have a lassi, too, only to find out how it tasted in Korea.

But there were many options when it came to non-vegetarian food as there were several items tagged under seafood, chicken and lamb.

I would not be critical of the food at Ganga as I finally got to taste Indian food after my ordeal in Incheon. Just eating the kind of food I wanted to have was enough for me and I couldn't be asking for more. There was a double reason for my happiness as I also managed to secure a table for myself in the nick of time. I reached there much before 7.30pm and was very conscious that I had to vacate the table by 8pm, as the Koreans are very punctual.

All's well that ends well. As I settled my bill, I glanced at my watch. It was exactly 8pm. I came out of Ganga feeling amused and happy — amused because never before had I had to eat at a restaurant so hastily!

Global Desi's Platter, DNA, Jaipur

October 22, 2016

26

Vegan Food in Southeast Asia

While vegetarianism has been an intrinsic part of Indian culture, the concept of veganism takes it a step ahead — one has to let go of all dairy products. I wouldn't be able to say whether it is a fad or something that will endure for years, but many well-known personalities across the globe have already turned vegetarian or vegan. Many new-generation actors have also confessed to have turned vegan. Even in western countries, many have changed their eating habits and have turned green for the sake of their health and the environment.

Maybe all this is for the better. Even in countries like South Korea, where meat consumption is high, or Malaysia, which is the melting pot of different cultures, vegetarian restaurants or vegan restaurants are opening up. In Malaysia, because of a large chunk of the population hailing from South India, it is understandable to find vegetarian or vegan restaurants. For example, all the joints serving South Indian dishes like dosas and *vadas* will not have anything to do with animal foods. Even the popular Saravana Bhavan, which is part of an international chain of vegetarian restaurants, is found in Kuala Lumpur. There are several vegetarian joints in Brickfields — also known as Little India of Kuala Lumpur.

Recently, I have begun to notice exclusive vegan places also making their mark. Water Lily Vegetarian Restaurant is a vegetarian restaurant turned vegan. Interestingly, there are dishes mentioned in the menu as meat or fish but actually they happen to be alternatives — purely vegetarian items. Then there is a Chinese Buddhist vegan restaurant called Natural Vegetarian Food Centre. Green Garden Organic is another vegan place that serves organic food, mostly seasonal and local produce. The best part is that it is not only an onion-free, garlic-free place, but also does not use monosodium glutamate (MSG) or ajinomoto, as it is commonly called.

Another name that comes to mind is the Dharma Realm Guan Yin Sagely Monastery — very close to the famous mall KLCC, which offers a buffet spread of around 15 dishes. The place also holds a chanting ritual-cum-ceremony in which the public can participate.

I have not been to all of these but here I cannot help mentioning The Ganga Café, which has earned the tag of the 'best vegetarian restaurant in Kuala Lumpur'. Their specialty is Gujarati cuisine and Malaysian fusion veggies. The owner is Meetha, who welcomes guests herself and takes care of them personally. This place also uses fresh vegetables from their own farm and their food is MSG-free.

In Seoul, one can come by quite a few vegan places. The Gwa Char is an abbreviation for 'rice with herbal medicine, fruit and vegetables'. They serve a vegan buffet and the food is prepared in a traditional manner with ingredients from small farms. Loving Hut is part of an international chain of vegan restaurants opened by followers of Supreme Master Ching Hai, an advocate for a vegan lifestyle.

Oh Se Gae Hyang is a 60-seater vegan restaurant owned by well-known Korean vegetarian food company, Vegifood. The place has a Korean-style seating with each of its 12 tables having a picture of a saint along with an aphorism associated with them.

The wave of vegan lifestyle will take a lot many years to enter the common man's home and I cannot even say for sure whether it will. However, I must note that veganism is not restricted to food only as vegan cosmetics are also entering the market nowadays. Interesting times ahead!

Global Desi's Platter, DNA, Jaipur

November 5, 2016

27

Rajasthani Touch in Japan

It is said that there are five types of countries in the world — developed, under-developed, developing, Argentina and Japan. We all know about the first three, but Argentina is an example of its own. It is rich in everything possible — minerals, good soil, water, but nobody can explain its disasters. Japan, on the other hand, had nothing after the atomic bombing and still it gives competition to any developed country.

My first visit to Japan was when I got a scholarship and was invited to study at the AOTS Institute. When I was in Japan, tandoori preparations were very popular and they still are.

There were many Indian restaurants in the Japanese cities of Tokyo, Osaka, Nagoya and Kyoto. Usually, I go to Indian restaurants in foreign countries in search of Indian people with whom I can converse in Hindi. But in the four evenings that I visited Osaka's two restaurants — Khajuraho and Delhi — I did not find any Indian faces.

During my stay in Japan, I saw only a few non-resident Indians at the Indian Embassy. Unlike the United States or Europe, where I could often spot Indian faces in the crowd, Japan did not offer me any such luck.

One evening I was walking along the road when a strange thing caught my eye. I could see a Pakistani flag fluttering in the wind, and on its reverse side, I saw our Tricolour. I moved closer to the flag and found it was mounted atop a restaurant named Gandhi. I entered the place in anticipation of meeting some fellow Indians, but to my dismay, I only found Japanese and Italians there, as usual.

The owner, Rafeeq Mengrani, welcomed me in traditional Japanese style and informed me that he had come to Japan from Pakistan two years ago. As Rafeeq was speaking to me, the cook came out. His name was Mangal Gujaar and he was from Rajasthan's Sikar district. When I told him I was from Rajasthan too, he was very happy. He was all the more excited because he could speak in his native language with someone after so long, having moved to Japan seven years ago. He confessed that he felt he had forgotten his mother tongue altogether.

Mangal prepared a sumptuous vegetarian meal especially for me. With all the magnificent dishes that Mangal offered, I felt at home. I forgot about how a little while ago I had felt sad at not seeing Indians in the country. I was relieved that I could finally converse in my native language, with Mangal on this foreign soil, while having wonderful Indian food.

I learnt from the deputy ambassador, Biren Nanda, that there were about 400 Indian restaurants in Japan. This was years ago in 1998, when I had visited the country. Many more Indian restaurants have come up since, including Shivam. Although I have not been there myself, I would like to visit Shivam the next time I go to Tokyo, having heard so much about it from my vegetarian friends. Shivam was started by a Jain businessman who basically needed to eat Jain food in Tokyo and therefore resolved to cater to more Jains like himself.

Global Desi's Platter, DNA, Jaipur

November 19, 2016

28

From Darjeeling to Bombay

We all know that Indian food is so popular abroad that you can only compare it to the popularity of Chinese food in India (to an extent). Now, of course, other kinds of cuisines are also gaining popularity, like Thai and Italian. One also finds some good Japanese specialty restaurants in India but it is yet to be universally accepted.

Indian food abroad mostly tastes quite different from what it tastes like in our own country. That is perhaps because of the fact that one has to keep in mind the local taste and modify according to their palate. Take, for example, Chinese food in India that tastes better than the original cuisine in China. Authentic Chinese food seems somewhat bland and tasteless compared to the food that is available in India. This is what I meant when I said tastes need to be modified according to the local palate, for acceptance.

There are a large number of Indian restaurants in Japan, particularly in big cities like Tokyo and Osaka.

Restaurants with names so varied — from Ashoka and Priya to Darjeeling and Gurgaon to some names with a Japanese touch, like Shinjuku Bombay.

Talking of names, I honestly think one should be sensitive in naming restaurants or any other organisation. In Tokyo, I visited a restaurant called Ganga. There was no harm in doing so as it is a common name associated with India. But I was shocked when I found that a restaurant with such a revered name serves not only alcohol, but also beef. In fact, a speciality dish mentioned is beef with naan. I do not have much belief in different customs and have often taken a stand against various ills passed on as customs, like dowry and so on. I also consider myself entirely secular, but even I was aghast and could not accept this conflation of the name Ganga with beef and alcohol.

On the other hand, there is Deva café in Tokyo that only serves vegetarian items. The dishes have names that are unmistakably clear and do not confuse guests with the nature of food served. Yogi Burger, among other things, is a hot favourite. There is also Nataraj, with its holy name, that lives up to its image. It is an Indian vegetarian restaurant with three outlets. The chef is named Sadanand and here any vegetarian can eat without fear of spoiling his meal.

My write-up would be incomplete without mentioning

the Vege Herb saga. This restaurant came up when I visited Japan for the first time.

Sometimes, I feel whatever items we eat at lavish weddings and so-called fancy restaurants only give a feel-good factor to our cuisine, without substantially amplifying its reach and connection. If that is not true, why are the humble chai and samosa the most popular Indian food items around the world?

Additionally, it intrigues me to think how India's food culture would have been transformed had certain items been equally appealing across the country. For example, think of samosa being a staple across South India just as they are in the North and dosas and idlis being the go-to food in North India besides their ubiquitousness in the South. Now, that would definitely put the seal on India's identity of being united in our diversity!

Global Desi's Platter, DNA, Jaipur

December 3, 2016

29

The Joy of *Chhola Bhatura* in Japan

Japan has given me a unique experience that I will cherish forever. My first visit to Japan was for a scholarship programme of the AOTS. The Association for Overseas Technical Scholarship (AOTS) was established in 1959 with the support of the Ministry of International Trade and Industry as the first technical organisation run entirely on a private basis in Japan. The main aim of AOTS is to promote international economic cooperation and enhance mutual economic development and friendly relationships between Japan and the rest of the world.

The main activities of AOTS include giving training to top management people of various developing countries in Japan, while exposing them to the Japanese industry and technology at the same time.

I was there for a management course and had to stay at the institute itself. I was absolutely sure I would not get any desi food in the institute or the canteen. As a result, the weight of the food items, including all kinds of pickles, *bhujia,* paratha etc that I was carrying in my baggage was far more than all the other stuff combined.

In the morning, after having paratha and pickles in my room — or may I call it a compartment, infamous as Japan is for its tiny living quarters — I decided to go to the canteen downstairs and have tea. As part of the scholarship, we were given a debit card that could be used in the canteen or other outlets within the institute.

In fact, while checking in at the institute, I saw the chocolate machine in the lobby and thought that my card would only be used for this purpose, as being a teetotaller, I would not use it in any bar. As for the canteen, I was sure that the card would not be of any use for their half-cooked rice and boiled noodles.

While entering the café, I was pleasantly surprised to smell Indian spices and with it, I started imagining things. Suddenly I saw the menu and read the words *chhola bhatura*; my joy knew no bounds.

Later, I gathered that for lunch and dinner, there is an Indian dish every day — since the students who come from India, Pakistan or Bangladesh always demand Indian food. Therefore, the institute decided to include Indian dishes on the menu.

The entry of Indian food happened 17 years before my maiden visit. During my entire stay at AOTS, I had my frozen parathas along with the Indian curries cooked by a Japanese chef who knew nothing about India. The desire of the students and the institution's decision made me believe that at the end of the day, one needs to have one's own cuisine to satisfy one's taste buds, and consequently, stimulate the intellect.

Global Desi's Platter, DNA, Jaipur

December 17, 2016

30

Junoon for Indian Taste in NY

My travels are invariably linked to food, the obvious reason being my search for Indian vegetarian food in a foreign land. My vegetarian palate has allowed me to taste all kinds of 'Indian' food — Indian in name, at least, although there could be several degrees of difference in taste.

New York has always been one of my favourite places where I could eat whatever I wanted. There are so many Indian restaurants and so many varieties to choose from. My frequent visits to Indian restaurants have also led me to make lots of friends and acquaintances.

With every visit to New York, I find more and more Indian eateries popping up, especially in the Lexington area and Long Island. While Tulsi and Junoon are very famous, there are a host of others, including Curry in a Hurry, Copper Chimney, Dhaba, Amma, The Masalawala, Benaras, Bhojan and many more.

Tulsi is a contemporary Indian cuisine eatery while Junoon serves traditional Indian food and is also bigger than Tulsi. I was not much impressed by the food at Junoon, although décor wise, it is certainly excellent.

The décor has a fine blend of Indian limestone with sandstone statues and antique wood carvings. It has three areas — Junoon Walk, Patiala Room and Spice Room. Junoon Walk is a 50-foot walkway with an impressive sandstone sculpture, The Tree of Life, that separates the two dining rooms. Patiala Room is named after Maharaja Bhupinder Singh of Patiala, whose love for extravagance was well-known, with the term 'Patiala peg' being attributed to him. This is a room with walnut flooring and innovative use of antique *jhoola* swings alongside glass-topped tables with an L-shaped bar. The Spice Room is the most interesting of them all, offering a view of all the different spices used in Indian cooking. It is in full public view, not only visually appealing to the diners, but also capable of whetting their appetites with the intoxicating aroma of fresh spices wafting in the air.

The person who showed me around the place was Walter D'Rozario, Junoon's chef de cuisine. Incredibly, I found a Kolkata connection with him, as he was born in Kolkata's Rawdon Street and used to live in the Tangra area!

The menu had some strange-sounding cocktails, ranging from Mumbai Margarita to Tandoori Tequila, Adraki Punch to Punjabi Passion, obviously to prove their Indian-ness. The lunch and dinner menus were separate, although a number of dishes were common.

From *missi roti* to *lachha paratha*, *mirchi pakora* to Lal Mirch ka Paneer, and kulfi to *phirni*, there seemed to be the usual favourites, along with clichéd ones like *dal makhani* and biryani.

The name Junoon means passion and the restaurant definitely tries to prove its culinary passion at every step.

As I did not find too many Indian service staff at Junoon, it was difficult to make them understand the kind of food I was looking for. This place was clearly not meant for Indians so much as it was for westerners eager for a mouthful of India.

Nevertheless, Junoon is easily one of the better-known and better-reviewed Indian eateries in New York. Its wine collection is hailed for its extensive stock, with an experienced sommelier available at all times to guide diners about the best wines to complement their dishes.

Global Desi's Platter, *DNA*, Jaipur

January 7, 2017

31

The *Malai* (Cream) of New York

Malai Marke — what an oddly appropriate name for a restaurant! A term associated with food alone, it encapsulates the punch of extra flavour. It is the perfect name for an Indian restaurant where Indian diners can be transported to Mumbai or Kolkata or Delhi simply by associating with the term — though strictly speaking, *malai marke* originally refers to tea with an extra dollop of cream.

I visited Malai Marke in 2015 when I was invited by a United Nations Association (UNA) official to dine out. I was in New York for my UNA meeting, and as my love for Indian food was well known, the restaurant was chosen keeping my tastes in mind. It is located on 318 East 6th Street — an area lined with several other Indian joints.

From the outside, it appears to be a nondescript place, just another Indian restaurant with the usual dishes on the menu. Despite the simple façade, I was quite surprised when I saw the place fully occupied on a Monday evening. It was evident that the food appealed to the western palate as the diners were all non-Indians.

I was not very impressed by the vegetarian fare that I tasted, it was nothing extraordinary — just about okay. My host clarified that the place is better-known for its non-vegetarian fare.

The founder of Malai Marke was Shiva Natarajan. He was, in fact, an illustrious restaurateur, behind several other eateries like Chote Nawab, Bhojan and Dhaba. Natarajan lived in Kolkata for many years before coming to the US to pursue a degree in business. However, he became a restaurateur when he realised that Indian regional cuisine was not well represented. That gave birth to a restaurant like Malai Marke, where many uncommon Indian regions also found their place on the menu. The result was a wide variety of dishes representing the best of the Indian gastronomic map.

Coondapur Kori (chicken) or Lal Maas may be among the favourite non-vegetarian dishes but the names that amused me were Aunt Murli's Chingri Malai Curry, Bhindi Sasuralwali, Chowrangi Aloo Dum (Chowringhee is a place in central Kolkata), Dhabewali Biryani and Tangra style Calcutta Chinese Specials, each dish laced with bags of nostalgia for Indians living away from home.

Ragda Patties, Paneer Khurchan and Bhindi Sasuralwali with naan and complimentary poppadom (papad) were the items that I tasted, and as I said earlier, they were not bad, they tasted okay to my Indian taste buds. All the same, I would heartily recommend people, especially non-vegetarians, to drop by at Malai Marke, if only to sample the tremendous variety of dishes that is served at the restaurant.

Global Desi's Platter, DNA, Jaipur

February 11, 2017

32

The Indian Lotus Blooms in New York

I first went to this Indian restaurant called Tamarind in 2012, located in the main city of New York, but returned less than impressed. In 2015, when Rajiv Mehta, a doctor and hotelier who is originally from Rajasthan, invited me for dinner at another Tamarind, this one located in the Tribeca area, a different part of the city, I was simply floored.

I gathered that the owner, Avtar Walia, had a restaurant in the Flatiron section of Manhattan (the one that I had visited earlier) and the new one was called Tamarind Tribeca, at 99 Hudson Street on Franklin Street. The new restaurant took architect Wid Chapman more than a year to build. Set in a handsome art deco building, this modern 11,000 square foot venue seats 175 people. Its two levels comprise the main dining room, a windowed bar and cocktail lounge on the first floor and a 1,500 square foot mezzanine. The entire space is flooded with natural light, thanks to almost 100 feet of windows throughout the restaurant.

Tamarind was awarded Michelin star status in 2012. The restaurant boasts of a lot of Hollywood diners, including Richard Gere, Woody Allen and Harrison Ford. The Clinton family is also said to favour Tamarind. Mr Walia, I learnt, has employed several chefs from across India for his restaurant to home in on the authentic flavours. Under the direction of Peter Beck, the restaurant's executive chef, the cuisines offered cover a vast range — Punjab, Goa, Hyderabad, Chennai, Kolkata and Lucknow are well represented.

In the late 1970s, Walia worked at the city's Tandoor restaurant as a captain and bartender. Later, he became the manager of Akbar restaurant on Park Avenue, which is when he thought of opening a fine dining establishment himself. Walia realised his dream by becoming the co-owner of the popular Daawat restaurant. Fifteen years later, he opened Tamarind on East 22nd Street, focusing his knowledge, passion and imagination to launch a world-class dining outlet. The experience and expertise of running a fine dining restaurant culminated in the launch of Tamarind Tribeca.

Anchoring the dining room at the restaurant site is

a tandoor kitchen with glass walls and a ceiling-high black metal roof. A wide range of materials and shapes has been used to create imaginative and original lighting throughout.

This restaurant is worth trying for its delicious food and ambience. Although it specialises in non-vegetarian dishes like Lobster Masala — its signature dish — I found a good variety of vegetarian items as well. Among the tandoor items is Pudinewala Paneer and Tandoori Sabzi, consisting of *palak* and paneer *tikkis,* along with a variety of vegetables.

Among Tamarind's special dinner options is Raji's Vegetarian Thali, which has vegetable kebabs, dal, *sabzi,* chutney, *puris* and rice. Sabzi Ke Bag Se, the vegetarian specialty section, has dishes like Dum Aloo Gobi, Raseele Aloo, Chana Pindi, Saag Paneer, Nargisi Kofta, Achari Khumb, Majjiga Pulusu (a South Indian item), among several others. Rosemary Naan, wild mushrooms and Truffle Oil Naan are additional items to delight the taste buds.

One of the most interesting features about this place is the Lotus Room, celebrating India's national flower. The private dining room at Tamarind Tribeca has been transformed into the Lotus Room, where lunch and tea are served daily from 11.30am to 5pm.

The award-winning chefs have also created a menu featuring several dishes prepared with lotus. For instance, there is a spinach kofta, which has lotus roots in it, and *jalpari,* which has lotus fries. One can also opt for lotus chip cookies to accompany their variety of teas — sourced from China, Assam, Darjeeling and Ceylon.

Global Desi's Platter, DNA, Jaipur

February 26, 2017

33

NY's Kolkata Connection

'In Curry Hill a New Kid on the Block' is how *The New York Times* referred to Haldi when it first opened in New York. While they serve Indian and Indo-Chinese, it is also interesting to see that they serve Tangra-style Chinese food. To those not familiar with this term, Tangra happens to be an area in Kolkata that houses a predominantly Chinese population. The Chinese in Tangra run food joints, have tanneries and celebrate Chinese festivals with gusto.

While Haldi — meaning turmeric in Hindi — seems an unusual name for a restaurant, it denotes Indian food, or broadly speaking, the food of the sub-continent, with turmeric being an essential ingredient. Being an Indian restaurant, one expects a variety of pan-Indian items at Haldi, but the interesting bit is the presence of a few Jewish dishes like Bamia Khuta (chicken with okra) or Chicken Makmura, a Kolkata Jewish specialty.

A glance at the menu and I know why this is different

from others. They have something called a 'small plate' that means food in small proportions. This is really convenient for diners who arrive alone or want to experiment with a new dish. Needless to say, it is pocket-friendly, too.

Upon surveying the menu, I noticed a clear tilt towards Kolkata. Apart from the Kolkata-Tangra connection, there are delicacies like Hawker Fish Fry Kolkata style, Alur Dum Kolkata style, Chor Chori, Mangshor Chop, Kosha Mangsho and Chingri Malai Curry, among the more common Indian dishes. The Kolkata connect became even more pronounced when I found *jhaal muri* — the quintessential Kolkata street food — and egg rolls being served. The rum balls too are reminiscent of the legendary Flurys of Kolkata.

The Indian vegetarian section has Methi Matar Malai, Paneer Makhani, Malai Kofta, Dal Makhani, Baingan Bharta and Bhindi Maa Ki (okra, mother's style), among a few other things. But my favourite was the dal Mathur himself prepared for us.

I had already heard that Mathur was no longer with Tulsi. One day, while walking along Lexington Avenue, the board of Haldi caught my eye and I thought of Mathur instantaneously as I had heard of his association with this eatery. The moment I looked through the glass window, I found him looking back at me. That is how we reconnected.

Mathur updated me that after leaving Tulsi, he is now the executive chef at Haldi and is also responsible for other places like Chola, Kokam, Chote Nawab, Dhaba, and Malai Maarke.

The chef treated us to dal — a mix of five lentils that was superb and bore his inimitable stamp. I came out happy, having found a slice of Kolkata in the heart of New York.

Global Desi's Platter, DNA, Jaipur
March 11, 2017

34

Carrying Forth the Bukhara Legacy

Bukhara Grill was the first Indian restaurant in New York that I had visited many years ago. The restaurant had catered to a number of foreign dignitaries, including the Indian Prime Minister. My first visit was more out of curiosity as Bukhara of ITC Maurya in Delhi is one of my all-time favourite eating places. So, it was the name that actually drew me to that place.

The food was good and the place was known to be vegetarian-friendly. In particular, their tandoor items were superb.

Bukhara Grill has become quite a hot spot because of its location, despite being a bit on the expensive side. It has managed to remain top of the charts because of its delicious food. I visited this triplex eatery once more last summer, to host a luncheon in their small banquet. The food tasted as delightful as it had the first time round.

My first visit there was with my finance officer of the

World Federation of United Nations Association (WFUNA) and we ordered quite a few varieties of kebabs. The lunch began with Subz Seekh Kebab and Dahi Aloo Papdi. Though the outlet is hailed as vegetarian-friendly, I found a majority of their tandoori items were non-vegetarian. The only two remaining items were grilled vegetables and Pudina Paneer Tikka. I really liked the dishes as the veggies were served hot, along with pineapple. It was 'delightfully different,' just as the dish was described in the menu. A non-vegetarian starter was named Sharabi Kebabi, but I am not in a position to say whether consuming the kebab made one tipsy!

For the main course, it had to be Dal Bukhara, along with Kurkuri Bhindi, Palak Bhutta and Aaj *ka* Aloo, chef's favourite of the day. Choosing the rice and roti was quite a task, with a seemingly endless variety of both on offer. Apart from naan, *kulcha* and rotis, there were different kinds of breads like Jalebi Paratha, Naan Toorewala and a special stuffed bread.

The Lunch Special section for vegetarians was a platter that included two vegetable curries, lentils, basmati pulao, naan and a green salad. I, however, chose to order individual dishes from the à la carte menu.

Desserts are something I need to avoid but end up eating anyway, especially if I find my favourite items on the menu. There were some exotic-sounding ones like Tilla Kulfi and Jamun-e-gul — a kind of light pastry made from milk and honey — and Shakori Rasmalai. Ice cream, sorbet and baklava (Middle Eastern pastry) were also there among the dessert options.

Overall, I came out quite satisfied with the quality of food and service and I can even say that the owners' association with the original Bukhara has paid off as they continue to carry forward the Bukhara legacy. With the kind of visitors that have set foot in this place — from Indra Nooyi and Sachin Tendulkar to Shashi Tharoor and more — it is clear what kind of reputation and popularity the Bukhara Grill has earned for itself over the years.

The best part is that they don't mind going out of their way to serve some vegetarian stuff that is not on the buffet menu when they realise you are not eating non-veg food. And, of course, for everything else, restaurateur Vicky Vij is always there with his smiling face and warm handshake!

Bukhara is a place where I host my regular get-togethers in New York as it is close to the UN as well.

Global Desi's Platter, DNA, Jaipur

March 25, 2017

35

The Curious Tale of a New York Dhaba

Dhaba is a ubiquitous word in India that conjures up the image of a simple, roadside eatery — open 24x7 — where people sit on cots, sip hot chai, and eat rotis and *dal tadka* fresh from the *chulha* (earthen stove). These, as you know, were once set up for truck drivers who could park their vehicles outside the eateries, have their meals and rest for a while. So, whenever one sees an eatery suffixed with 'dhaba', one knows what kind of food to expect there.

I am now going to talk of a dhaba set not in India, but thousands of miles away from the homeland, in the United States. Yes, this particular dhaba is in the heart of New York. Of course, this dhaba is a far cry from its Indian counterparts.

This dhaba is on Lexington Avenue amidst a whole lot of other eateries. I understand they have about 125 items on their menu. In keeping with the name, the menu claims to have Dhaba Ka Chawal and Dhabawali Rotiyan. They serve food that is commonly termed as street food. The *pav* section includes famous butter buns from Mumbai and has items like *vada pav* and *pav bhaji* — the typical street food of Maharashtra. Thelawala chats have *bhel puri, paani puri,* Purani Delhi ki Papri Chaat, *chhola bhatura* and others. Several types of naan, paratha, *poori, kulcha* and rotis are available. The dal section also offers a variety, including *rajma* and Dhaba Dal Makhani.

A section called British Curry House reads: 'Modelled after dishes that are popular on the other side of the pond', where 'curry' has become more of a staple than a fancy. These curries have a unique Anglo-Indian flavour. Curry, ironically enough, is traditionally a term that is non-existent in the Indian culinary landscape and was used originally by the British in colonial India to mean anything with a spicy gravy.

In India, one may find people surreptitiously drinking beer or whisky at dhabas, but this being the West, how could an eating place, even a dhaba, not serve a variety of drinks? Unsurprisingly, there were all the drinks that one could think of, including a number of cocktails. What caught my eye was the Highway Lassi, which was not our own desi version, but a cocktail of mango, yogurt, champagne and tequila. Certain clichés were perhaps unavoidable. Talking of India, there had to be Kamasutra

— a drink of vodka, rum and gin with strawberries and mango.

I had ordered some food online and found the menu good enough. I would not say it was extraordinary to the Indian palate, but it was fairly good. I heard mixed reviews about the place — some raved about it whereas some found it ordinary. But I read the review of *The New York Times,* which was very reasonable. The reviewer liked its Tale Huye Caju (fried cashews) but recommended that it was better not to have the desserts.

My interest in the place was piqued by my curiosity about what kind of food a dhaba in the West was likely to serve. So here I was, eating dhaba food in New York amidst urban folks!

Global Desi's Platter, DNA, Jaipur

April 8, 2017

36

Flavours from Sindh in New York

Kailash Parbat, the very Indian-sounding name, belongs to a New York restaurant that specialises in Indian cuisine. I usually dine at Indian restaurants with North Indian specialty. But I decided to try this place for its USP — *chaat.* And having tried it once, which was four years ago, it has since been a must-visit for me in New York.

I had been hearing about this place for a long time but could not get a chance to visit it earlier. The present owners are the third generation running the show. Their grandfather opened the first Kailash Parbat in Mumbai after coming from Pakistan following Partition. Since then, they have opened branches in several cities of India. Apart from the one in New York, there is one in London and another one in Singapore, too.

This upscale Lexington Avenue restaurant hardly reflects the history of hardship and struggle faced by the owners' forefathers. Prior to Partition, the Mulchandanis sold *pani puri* in Karachi. In 1952, they came to India, leaving their valuables behind and bringing only their utensils to make their specialty fare. Over the years, the roadside *halwai* of Colaba became one of the iconic eateries of Mumbai.

The best thing about this place is that it is purely vegetarian. Naturally, a person like me would be able to eat here without much thought. I came to have *chaat* here before heading to Haldi. I also had *gol gappas* aka *pani puris* aka *phuchka*, which were, no doubt the 'melt-in-the-mouth' kind that the restaurant boasts of. There was a *chaat* bar, where one could mix the ingredients to one's liking and have it.

Apart from *bhel puri, dahi vada, samosa, tikia* and *papri chaat,* the eatery offers *chhola bhatura, pav bhaji,* Mumbai *vada pav,* and *ragda patties* — all typical Mumbai specialties. The KP Chaat Platter is an assorted platter of *chaat* including *bhel puri, dahi vada,* corn basket and Khatte Meethe Aloo – all for less than $15. Some of the items tagged under Sindhi cuisine are *Bhee Ki Tikki* (lotus root), *sai bhaji* and *seyal paneer.*

Kailash Parbat also serves what they call Indo-Chinese, keeping in mind the popularity of Chinese food. I was quite fascinated by a dish called *koki*, which is a favourite Sindhi delight — spiced roti served with dahi, pickle and papad. I would definitely like to try it out sometime alongside some other Sindhi specialties.

The eatery serves Kulfi Falooda, which the owners claim to be a specialty since 1952 — the year of its inception. I noticed their website carries the word 'kosher' and there is also an endorsement certificate from a rabbi to prove its veracity. The restaurant, which opened in 2014, has since got pretty good reviews. *The New York Times* says, "Mumbaikars were giddy about the April opening of a Murray Hill outpost Kailash Parbat, a South Mumbai institution that is famous for its vegetarian *chaat*, or street snacks, many of which have their origins in the Sindh region, which is now part of Pakistan."

Talking of an Indian restaurant, one cannot do without lassis or masala chai — no matter whether it is a Punjabi or a Sindhi restaurant, or any other. This one is no exception.

So, when in New York, if you are itching to have some *chatpata chaat* — authentic and cheap — look no further. Head straight to Manhattan's Kailash Parbat.

Global Desi's Platter, DNA, Jaipur

April 22, 2017

37

Bollywood in the Big Apple

If there is one thing India has successfully exported all over the planet, it is undoubtedly Bollywood. Our stars and films have captured the hearts of millions of non-Indians, who even claim to be obsessive fans of certain actors. If one wants to strike up a conversation with a stranger, I feel Bollywood films can be a good starting point.

It was not surprising that I came across an Indian restaurant in New York by the name of Chote Nawab. The duo of Shiva Natarajan and, of course, Hemant Mathur, was behind this place too, as is the case with most other good Indian restaurants here. The former hails from Kolkata and became a restaurateur instead of pursuing his management career. In 2015, Natarajan sold his Indian restaurants in New York City to Michelin star chef Mathur to write a cookbook and brand his own sauces. Mathur, on the other hand, hails from Jaipur but worked in Delhi and Kolkata before moving overseas. The star status that he has earned in the US is in no small part due to his indefatigable dedication and passion for cooking. Mathur has earned numerous accolades and a sterling reputation, including the designation of 'Tandoor Master' and the title of 'the Yo-Yo Ma of tandoor cooking'.

And now back to Chote Nawab on Lexington Avenue, to sample the magic of Indian cuisine. The décor is kitschy, perhaps deliberately so, in keeping with the Bollywood theme. On entering, I was greeted by what looked like the big poster of a film called *Chote Nawab*, but was actually wall art. The several paintings on the wall reminded one of the rustic images commonly associated with India, strikingly lifelike in their appearance. The walls are bold and bright, with colourful ceramic plates stuck on them.

The name of the restaurant is a clue to the cuisine, its focus being on exclusivity. The food is quite princely, to say the least. The USP of the place is kebabs and *dum* dishes, as I gathered. The lunch menu is always minimal and the price is relatively less, too, compared to the more elaborate dinner menu.

Dishes from all the erstwhile princely states like Lucknow, Hyderabad, Mangalore and Kashmir are well-represented. Apart from the kebabs on the à la carte menu, there are two kebab platters for vegetarians and non-vegetarians each, served with spinach, rice, naan or roti. The name Bade Miya Peshkash caught my eye, which said 'our favourite kebabs from the tandoor'.

I began with appetisers like Baingan Dahiwala and Lucknowi Paneer Tikka. For the main course, there was the mischievously sounding Dal Mein Kala (*kali dal*), Nimboo Paneer, Bhindi Sasuralwali (the name was explained too!) and Baghara Baingan Mirch Ka Salan accompanied by naan and Burhani Raita. I gave the desserts a miss. I was tempted to try the gulab jamuns but had a mango lassi instead.

My friend tried out some other dishes but the most interesting was 'phall' — a British Indian curry that had numerous types of chillies. His feedback on his orders, which was mostly non-vegetarian, was quite positive. I was happy with the dishes I chose and, overall, I would say it was an interesting culinary experience. A rather regal one at that!

Global Desi's Platter, DNA, Jaipur

May 6, 2017

38

Indian Taste — Delhi or NY?

Last week, I visited the much talked-about restaurant in New Delhi called Indian Accent. The restaurant is located in a posh area of Friends Colony. Given the restaurant has been hit by the new law of the government that mandates no liquor within 500 metres of highways, I presumed they will have enough tables to accommodate walk-ins. But my butler at ITC Maurya informed me that it's as busy as Bukhara, and, to my surprise, the restaurant was packed to capacity even for a 7pm slot.

I was quite impressed with the quality of food and I was fortunate enough to get a chance to interact with the executive chef. Honestly, the interaction with him has cleared the not-so-good feeling I brought back from the Indian Accent restaurant in New York.

Indian Accent on 123W 56th Street in New York claims that it offers an inventive approach to Indian cuisine. In 2016, when I was in New York, I went to this restaurant at the Le Parker Meridien Hotel, when it had just opened.

I had heard a lot about the restaurant run by restaurateur Rohit Khattar. The original Indian Accent came up in New Delhi in 2009 and earned global recognition as India's finest dining place. The new place in New York had become operational just about four months prior to my visit. It was a little difficult to get a table at two days' notice, but by the same afternoon, I managed to get confirmation.

It is quite common at hyped-up Indian restaurants all over the world that when you call to book a table, they glibly say, 'it is full' and then, hours, or sometimes days later, you get a call back informing you of your table. I have noticed this trend with many Indian restaurants in Dubai, Bangkok and London as well.

But Indian Accent was a full house when I got there and there weren't any other Indians in the restaurant. Apart from the hostess and a couple of senior staff members, I did not find any Indians serving food. Given the non-Indian footfall, it is no surprise that Indian Accent has also created a few dishes especially for New Yorkers, including beef items.

The décor of the 60-seater restaurant can best be described as minimalist, designed by Rohit's wife Rashmi in collaboration with designers BHDM to give a modern look. The restaurant's chef is Manish Mehrotra, also a partner of Khattar.

Regarding their cuisine, the restaurant's website writes that Chef Manish Mehrotra 'reinterprets nostalgic Indian dishes with an openness towards global techniques and influences.' As in most other places, this restaurant too has separate menus for lunch and dinner. In reality what it means is that essentially both menus are the same but the lunch menu is a truncated version. There are menu cards with a section called Chef's Tasting, apart from the regular à la carte. The pricing is pre-fixed, depending on the number of courses. A seven-course Chef's Tasting lunch costs $75.

The dinner is more elaborate, with more variations. A look at the menu reconfirmed my opinion that it is more suitable for the western palate. Some of the items that could easily be termed as 'experimental' are *kulchas* with wild mushroom, Pumpkin Cheddar, Butter Chicken, Hoisin Duck and Pastrami Mustard. Or the desserts, like Cheeni Ki Roti, Marshmallows and Old Monk Ice Cream. Also, part of the Chef's Tasting offerings are Kashmiri Morels, walnut powder and Parmesan Papad. Far from a conventional Indian line-up.

I did have a meal at the Indian Accent in New York, but

honestly, my desi taste buds were not satisfied. Although the meal, costing around $100, was more than enough to fill my belly, it wasn't good enough to do justice to the essence of an Indian meal.

How can you define Indian food without roti, naan or rice? A three-course $100 meal in this restaurant does not include Indian breads and rice because, as they (at the Indian Accent) say, they serve "modern Indian cuisine."

However, I do not wish to discourage people from dining here, as their original counter in New Delhi has earned a formidable reputation and is doing pretty well. Perhaps, one should dine in both the New Delhi and New York restaurants to compare the taste and decide for themselves the relative merits of the 'inventive approach' to Indian cuisine.

Global Desi's Platter, DNA, Jaipur
May 20, 2017

39

A Bombay Experience in London

Indian food journeys in London cannot begin with any restaurant other than the one that has an unmistakable Indianness in the name itself — Bombay Brasserie.

This famous restaurant on Courtfield Road, Kensington, that has been operational since 1982 attracts the glitterati, politicians and industry barons alike. It's perhaps the only Indian restaurant in London whose address every Indian knows by heart. The menu is a mix of Mumbai's cultural diversity comprising influences from Parsi, Goan, Gujarati, Bengali, as well as Portuguese and the Raj cuisines.

"Back in 1982, Bombay Brasserie was created around the idea of bringing the cuisine of this great city to London and today's menus reflect this ongoing exploration, featuring the freshest seafood, chicken, lamb and game, plus plenty to please vegetarian palates.... Our menus feature a wide variety of cooking techniques, from slow-cooked curries to grills and kebabs as well as tandooris from the clay oven."

A description of the restaurant in its own words (on its website).

A weekend brunch with *paani puri* and *bhel* — quintessential Bombay foods — is served at a live *chaat* counter every Saturday and Sunday and is quite popular. Apart from the set lunch and dinner menus, there is the à la carte menu that offers a wide variety of dishes with all the distinctive culinary influences. Besides the *batata puri* and *palak chaat* in the starters, there are some unique-sounding dishes like Chilli Milli Kebab that is explained as spiced vegetable cakes wrapped around a bullet chilli.

In the vegetarian fare, with the usual *baingan bharta* and *dal makhani*, one finds Chonkha Sabzi, which is stir-fried water chestnuts, beans, carrots, garden peas, bell peppers and roasted potatoes, and Adraki Gobhi. I could see a non-vegetarian Parsi dish, some *salli boti* and Kasundi Monkfish, explained as mustard from Kolkata.

I have not tasted the non-vegetarian food but with my frequent experience of dining in this restaurant as well as hosting several dinners here, I have been able to learn the names of many food items. I am in a position to identify in many cases which place a particular item belongs to. That Patrani Machchi is a common Parsi dish and venison roast a Goan item with definite Portuguese roots no longer needs to be told to me!

After starters like Palak Chaat and Chilli Milli Kebab,

I had Adraki Gobhi, Bhindi Amchuriya and Wadi Bhutta Palak, accompanied with Saffron Pulao and Peshwari Naan. I normally do not have desserts, but found some refreshingly sweet dishes like Jamun Kulfi, Rose Kulfi and Pista Phirni.

The executive chef of this restaurant used to be Prahlad Hegde, who had trained under the well-known chef, Hemant Oberoi, at the Taj Hotels, Mumbai. Since his childhood, Chef Prahlad had been interested in cooking and had helped his family in their own restaurants. In 1991, he joined Bombay Brasserie. He always chooses his ingredients himself and prepares all the spices in-house in order to bring the unique flavours of India to his dishes. Chef Prahlad's dedication to Indian cuisine and Bombay Brasserie, in particular, was recognised by *The Good Curry Guide*, which honoured him with a Lifetime Achievement Award.

At present, the reins of running the restaurant are in the able hands of award-winning chef Sriram Aylur, whose personalised interactions with the guests have contributed to its immense popularity and increased the number of diners in the restaurant, making it the ultimate destination for Indian food in the British capital. He also supports many charities through his culinary skills.

Global Desi's Platter, DNA, Jaipur

June 17, 2017

40

Dishoom in London

I went to this unique Indian restaurant in London called Dishoom for the very first time with Sir David Green. Apparently, a reservation at this restaurant is the first thing that Indian guests demand at the concierge desk in London hotels.

The visit to this restaurant was a rather nostalgic experience. Its ambience recreated the old-world charm of Mumbai's Irani restaurants. The dishes were truly from the old Bombay days. The word 'Dishoom' has a Bollywood connection – implying *masala* movies with a lot of fight sequences and the quintessential '*dishoom*' sound effects.

At the turn of the century, there were about 400 Irani cafes in Mumbai. Unfortunately, only less than 30 remain now. These were set up by Zoroastrians, commonly known as Parsis, who immigrated from Iran. These were cafes where students had breakfast, families dined, lawyers read briefs and writers found their characters. In other words, this was a place where people from all walks of life came to have their food and spend time.

Dishoom in London was founded in 2010 by Shamil and Kavi Thakrar and Amar and Adarsh Radia. It has pleased London diners with its presentation of modern Indian dishes with a twist. Alongside traditional meals like aromatic biryanis and the brunch dish Kejriwal (two fried eggs on chilli cheese toast) is its signature Bacon Naan Roll — a freshly baked naan with chilli-tomato jam, fresh herbs and smoked streaky bacon called The Ginger Pig.

'All Day, Every Day' is how Dishoom talks about its cuisine, starting with Bombay Breakfast, Lunch, Afternoon Chai, Dinner and Tipples. A few names need to be mentioned to elucidate its uniqueness. Kejriwal, which has been explained as a favourite of the Willingdon — the first such Bombay institution to admit natives — is reputedly named after a member who kept asking for it. Bombay Omelette, Akuri, Bun Maska and Fire Toast supplement the breakfast menu at Dishoom.

In the interesting all-day section, they serve a variety of dishes ranging from bhel, *pav*, samosa, *pav bhaji* — a Bombay staple — to kebabs, biryani, naan, dal and salad and a whole lot of other foods that can silence the rumbling stomach any time.

How can one talk of Bombay food without mentioning *kala khatta gola* — fluffy ice flakes with kokum syrup just as it is found on Chowpatty beach? Here, too, it is very much present with all the right ingredients.

What I particularly liked is the way Dishoom presents its menu, with a lot of consideration. The menu card separately lists dishes for children, and people with allergies to food items like dairy and gluten. Whether it is food or drinks, most of the offerings are explained to guests with a slice of Bombay. Take this for instance — 'first comes the marinade, then the open-air grill. Picture Bademiya in Colaba, a Bombay institution since 1942. A balmy night, with newspapers laid out on old car bonnets. You eat. Savour. Spill.'

Some of the different dishes I had were Gunpowder Potatoes, a grilled version of potatoes with aromatic seeds; Butter-Bhutta, a corn on the cob grilled on charcoal fire as on Chowpatty beach; and something called Gadbad Mitha — fresh fruits with custard and ice cream, which I had ordered simply because of its peculiar name.

When in London, I would request you to go and eat at one of Dishoom's several outlets to savour the taste of Irani dishes and get nostalgic about Bombay. I repeat — Bombay, not Mumbai.

I end this piece with the description of a drink, The

Dhoble, that is served here. "A refreshing breakfast cocktail, named after the notorious party-pooping Assistant Commissioner of Bombay Police, Vasant Dhoble. Fresh orange juice, Colombo gin, maraschino liqueur and a squeeze of lemon, served with cubed ice."

Global Desi's Platter, DNA, Jaipur

July 1, 2017

41

A Gymkhana Experience

Gymkhana is a word laden with colonial overtones. The original word is supposed to be *gendkhana*, meaning ball court. Gymkhana clubs used to be gentlemen's clubs during the British Raj. In the Indian subcontinent, one finds these gymkhana clubs in all major cities like Mumbai, Chennai, Delhi or Karachi and Lahore, to name a few.

It was thus very natural to find a place by the name of Gymkhana in London. Only in this case, it was a restaurant and not a club.

I went to the Gymkhana restaurant in London a couple of years ago with the London-based film-director and artiste, Sangeeta Datta. At that time, the restaurant featured on the top slot in the National Restaurant Award list of a leading Indian newspaper, beating the best of the British restaurants. Since this was the first time that a London restaurant had achieved such a feat, I decided to pay a visit. It was tough getting a reservation and I had to make a few phone calls to get one.

I went there with great expectations. Though an Indian restaurant, its food was not at all cut out for the Indian palate. Hence, my taste buds were not quite happy. The restaurant manager informed me that their chef was someone who had taught the craft to the chefs of the Benares restaurant in London. My earlier dining experience at Benares was not so pleasant either, with hardly any choice of desi Indian vegetarian food.

The restaurant décor at London's Gymkhana is really well done, though. The Gymkhana of the colonial era comes alive with dark wooden panelling, ceiling fans hanging from the top, cane furniture and a stack of hunting photographs in sepia tones — so very British!

The food at the place is described by the owner, Karan Sethi, as '*ghar ka khana, chatpata* and spicy'. I am listing some of the best dishes, in no particular order. There is Biryani of Wild Muntjac Deer, Pork Cheek Vindaloo, Quail Seekh Kebabs, Chettinad Duck, and their biggest hit, the Kid Goat Methi Keema to which the *bheja* can be added too. Now, all these dishes seemed Greek to me — both in terms of taste and names.

What I found interesting is the inclusion of the Hunter's Menu in their menu card. This has the typical dishes that were probably cooked with the meat of game hunted by sahibs in the bygone era. So, there are Pigeon Samosa,

Sofian Roe Deer Chop and the Muntjac Biryani that I have mentioned earlier.

I had some paneer tikka, corn *chaat*, Rajasthani Bhindi, Baingan ka Salan and beetroot chops *pav*, with rasmalai and apple *murabba* for dessert. There were other items like *gajar ka halwa*, pista kulfi and date and fig kheer.

I usually do not have much to talk about liquor as I do not understand much in this category. But I would like to talk about Gymkhana's drinks for a change. I found some uncommon names like Kaapi Martini, which had coffee liqueur and espresso. Brigadiers Blazer was also in sync with the Gymkhana culture. This cocktail happens to have rum with raspberries and blackberries.

As I have mentioned earlier, my desi taste buds wanted to try out the familiar flavours they are accustomed to, which, unfortunately, they were deprived of, as the food was perhaps prepared keeping British tastes in mind. However, this should not be a dampener as it is not a mean achievement for a restaurant to bag the most prestigious award in London. One should definitely visit the Gymkhana to savour the colonial food of India, albeit British style!

Global Desi's Platter, DNA, Jaipur

July 15, 2017

42

The French Connection

This column is different from my previous ones, as I am writing about Indian food with a difference this time — Indian food influenced by the French. The name of this London restaurant itself indicates its French connection. La Porte des Indes, when translated into English, means Gateway to India.

I was introduced to this restaurant by Baroness Verma and her husband, Ashok Verma, when they invited me to dinner there. Operational since 1996, this place specialises in Indo-French cuisine and the décor is inspired by the culture and style of Pondicherry, which was a French colony in the 19th century. The place, now called Puducherry, still bears the stamp of the French, and is revered by the devotees of Shri Aurobindo and Mirra Alfassa (the 'Holy Mother') as the former's ashram was situated there.

This restaurant is housed in a former Edwardian ballroom, spread over two floors, adorned with antique Indian artefacts and a white marble staircase, exotic plants and flowers, a 40-foot waterfall, a bar and private rooms.

The executive chef, Mehernosh Mody, served in the original La Porte des Indes in Brussels before joining the London restaurant. Prior to that, he worked with the Taj Group in New Delhi and Mumbai. He, along with his wife, spent time in Puducherry and spoke to the French people there, convincing them to part with their French-Creole recipes. This award-winning chef has written a book, conducts cooking classes where he shares his culinary secrets and also appears on television.

As one of London's premier specialty and fine dining restaurants, Las Porte des Indes has, over the years, been the proud recipient of a number of awards. It is one of the few restaurants in the city that has earned the appreciation of critics as well as connoisseurs.

Now for the main topic — food. The vegetarian that I am, Las Porte des Indes has an amazing array of dishes to suit my palate. Starters included Bombay Chaat, paneer kebab, *farsan* (meaning 'snacks' in Gujarati) items made of *besan* and *arbi* (colocasia) leaves, while the speciality was a classic from Pondicherry called Beignets d' Aubergines — fried aubergine roundels filled with a sensational cheese and herb pâté.

The main course gave us a lot of choice. From Punjabi Chhole, Bombay Aloo, Lotus Root Jaipuri, Nayantara Do

Piyaz, vegetarian biryani to Rougail d' Aubergines — smoked aubergine crushed with chilli, ginger and fresh green lime, another speciality from Pondicherry. Among the accompaniments, along with raita, naan and paratha, was Le Pain Creole — pan-fried lacy rice flour pancakes — yes, a Pondicherry speciality.

The dessert menu had ice cream, kulfi, kheer and coffee among other sweets and fruity items. Café du Pondicherry is featured among the coffees, too. After all, how could a French colony in South India not have its own version of coffee?

La Porte des Indes has been regularly applauded for its excellence. No wonder that the likes of Alec Baldwin, Goldie Hawn, Kylie Minogue, Leonardo DiCaprio, Robert Redford and Will Smith, to name only a few from the vast list of other high-profile visitors, keep flocking back.

I was simply bowled over by the restaurant's ambience, service and food. I would strongly recommend a visitor in London to dine here for an incredibly enriching experience.

Global Desi's Platter, DNA, Jaipur

July 29, 2017

43

Phahurat — Bangkok's Little India

Last month I was in Bangkok. Thailand and, in particular, the charming city of Bangkok, ranks among the most favourite international destinations for Indians. I think one of the reasons for this could be the presence of such a large number of Indians and, of course, the short distance from India.

One feels very comfortable in this foreign land. It is a common sight to spot turbaned Sikhs or women in salwar kameez. There are said to be more than 70,000 Sikhs in Thailand, most of whom stay in Bangkok. The first Sikh to migrate to Thailand was Ladha Singh in 1890. By 1911, many Sikh families had settled in Thailand. Bangkok was the centre of the migrant Sikhs. With the Sikh community's numbers rising, they decided to establish a gurdwara in 1912.

A wooden house was rented near Baan Moh, a well-known business area. In 1913, with the number of Sikhs in Bangkok continuing to rise, a new, larger wooden house was taken on a long-term lease near Phahurat. As time passed, in 1979, it was decided to renovate the gurdwara and make it bigger to accommodate the increasing number of Sikhs. The new gurdwara was completed after two years, in 1981.

Phahurat district, a large fabric market, is Bangkok's Little India, next door to Chinatown, a hub of the large Indian business community. Several textile shops can be seen here, mostly owned by Sikhs. The area that would become Phahurat was initially an enclave of Vietnamese immigrants who came to Siam during the reign of King Taksin (1767-1782).

In 1898, a fire broke out and paved the way for a road, which was named Bahurada by King Chulalongkorn in remembrance of his daughter, Princess Bahurada Manimaya, who had died at a young age. Today Bahurada is commonly spelled as Phahurat, or Pahurat.

Many of today's Phahurat residents are of South Asian descent. The Sikh community settled there more than a century ago and established a textile trading centre that is still thriving. The golden-domed Sri Guru Singh Sabha temple is a landmark of Phahurat.

For the average traveller, shopping in Phahurat may not

be very exciting. But for an Indian traveller — one who is steeped in Bollywood movies and loves desi stuff like paan or *mithai*, this is *the* place to be. If one is looking for fabrics, however, Phahurat is definitely not a place to be missed. And even if one is not too seriously looking for fabrics, it is still a great adventure to visit the Phahurat Fabrics Market. The first task is to actually find it — it seems to be carefully hidden and you need to walk through a couple of other stores to get into it. Thousands of retailers of Indian descent sell fabrics in every colour, shape and pattern that you could possibly imagine. Some shops specialise in custom-made wedding gifts, dresses and souvenirs.

This old market is a labyrinth of narrow lanes, barely wide enough for two people to pass simultaneously. The market has managed to hold on to its unique identity and character ever since it was founded. Besides fabrics, Phahurat is also an excellent place for buying accessories, such as trinkets and sandals. There are literally thousands of different kinds for sale, and all for a bargain. You'll also notice many stores selling religious paraphernalia like statues and pictures of Indian deities.

I have heard some strange stories about the Indians. The most interesting thing is that the Sikhs living in Thailand have started adopting Thai names. Younger generations of Sikhs living in Thailand are adopting Thai names along with their existing names for the sake of their national identity. They do this to give themselves a Thai identity and keep themselves on government records but at the same time also manage to cling to their Indian roots.

Around 70 percent of Sikhs in the country have Thai names and speak the Thai language. Those of the first generation of immigrants use Punjabi names, but the present generation uses both Sikh and Thai names. While most Sikhs are based in Bangkok, there are also some enclaves in Pattaya, Phuket, Hat Yai, Ubon, Udon, Pattani, Chiang Mai and Chiang Rai. The primary occupation of most of these Sikh families is trading, especially textile trading.

Even Sikh women have adopted Thai names for the sake of convenience. For example, a lady by the name Devinder Kaur Rajni would perhaps be called Rachnee. Although all official documents and schools have these Thai names, the people address each other by their original Sikh names. I once met a group of Thai Sikhs back home in India whose children study in Indian schools. I heard them talk among themselves in Thai and was quite astonished.

However, when they spoke to others in India, they spoke in Hindi, but with a peculiar Thai accent. It felt really strange to see a group of Sikh men and women speak in Thai among themselves, and also in Hindi with a Thai accent. These Thai Sikhs were not very fluent in English, and even when they spoke in English, they had the same Thai accent.

Seeing these turbaned Sikh men and salwar kameez-clad women in Thailand speak in Thai as well as Punjabi, visiting the gurdwara or carrying on their duties at these holy places, observing traditional customs during weddings makes me proud of our rich Indian culture. Even after living thousands of miles away from their motherland, settled in a foreign land for generations, this community has not relinquished its traditions.

Even though the new generations are more Thai, speaking a language that is a mixture of Thai and Punjabi, they are still tied to the land of their forefathers in a number of ways.

The bottom line is if you are in Bangkok, do go to Phahurat to soak in the culture of the local Sikhs — you can listen to their *shabad kirtan* and eat at their langar at the gurdwara, where you find local Sikh men and women working with immense devotion. The intensity of such devotion is in no way less than that of their counterparts in India.

The Asian Age

October 12, 2017

44

For a Quiet Durga Puja, Head Abroad

I have noticed that a lot of Indian festivals fall in the months of October and November. And I don't mean only Hindu festivals. People from different communities celebrate their festivals at this time. To start with, the Hindu festivals Navratri/Durga Puja/Dussehra, Kali Puja/Diwali and Chhath Puja are the most common. Of course, people have now started celebrating Lakshmi Puja and Jagadhatri Puja as well with a lot of gusto and fanfare. Celebrities from the film industry, especially Bollywood, come to Kolkata, and even to the suburbs, to inaugurate these pujas.

Jagadhatri Puja used to be a speciality of the erstwhile French colony of Chandannagar in Bengal, where idols would go up to 20 or 25 feet. But nowadays we see idols of Durga, Kali or Jagadhatri going up to such great heights in Kolkata itself. In this context, I remember a huge idol of

Durga about two years ago that was much publicised and caused a lot of problems to the police, and finally people were allowed a glimpse only from outside the gate.

Coming back to the celebrations, one finds Sikhs celebrating their biggest festival, Guru Nanak Jayanti, and observing Guru Nanak's birthday on Kartik Purnima, which they call Gurupurab. They take out big processions where they display their proficiency in sword-fighting or stick-fighting. The Jains too celebrate this day as Kartik Purnima. In Kolkata, the Jains take out a procession of Lord Parasnath. The idol is placed on a rath and taken to another temple. On this day, Jains go on a pilgrimage to worship Lord Adinath at his temple on Shatrunjaya Hills at Palitana in Gujarat. This Shatrunjaya Teerth Yatra is very important to Jain devotees, who cover a treacherous journey of 216 kilometres on rough mountainous terrain on foot to worship at the Lord Adinath temple atop the hill.

I recently came across a magazine article that talked about the Wangala Festival. This is a festival of Meghalaya's Garo tribe, also known as the Festival of 100 Drums, which is actually a harvest festival, observed to mark the onset of winter. The members of the tribe dress up in traditional vibrant outfits to pay obeisance to the Sun God and offer their thanks at the end of the sowing season.

The festivities are marked by blowing horns, traditional dance performances and, of course, the beating of drums.

During the Durga Puja/Navratri period this year, I was in Geneva, the second largest city of Switzerland. The two-day trip was for a United Nations meeting there. Most Indians living in Geneva work with NGOs as there are over 20 internationally renowned organisations there. Geneva is also the headquarters of the Red Cross (International Committee of the Red Cross) and the European base of the UN, as well as a global hub for diplomacy and banking.

On Ashtami, I saw Durga Puja being celebrated at the Centre Védantique Genève. I had earlier seen Durga Puja celebrated in Montreal, Quebec, and had heard of many Durga Pujas being held in Britain and the United States. In America, Durga Puja is organised in numerous places, which is hardly surprising as it is a vast country with a considerable presence of the Indian diaspora.

In fact, several pujas are held in places as far apart as Texas and Washington, and in New York, too, pujas are hosted by several organisations. There are many Bengali associations and cultural organisations that hold Durga Pujas, besides places like the Ramakrishna Mission centres.

Durga Puja as a community puja began in the 1970s in the US. Unlike in their motherland, here deities are not bought afresh every year as they are not immersed after the rituals are over. They are packed neatly into boxes and put away, to be taken out the following year again. The pujas here, unlike those back home, are celebrated in a restrained, traditional manner. There is no extravagance in décor or pandals, nor are there any of the modern trappings one finds in puja pandals in West Bengal these days.

The priest or *purohit* is usually flown in from India to conduct the pujas, which are organised in schools, churches or community centres. For cultural entertainment, we find the local Bengali community taking part with toddlers raised on foreign soil dancing to Bengali songs, which is always a wonderful sight! Of course, with more money pumped in and a large number of young professionals settled here, renowned singers and performers from Bengal are also invited to perform during this time.

The speciality of Durga Puja outside India is that it is celebrated on a weekend during the Puja dates or one that is closest to the Pujas. Unlike other festivals like Holi or Diwali, which are celebrated over a period according to convenience, and are flexible, Durga Puja is celebrated adhering to the actual dates. One sees Holi Milans and Diwali parties hosted by different outfits on different dates, both in India as well as abroad.

To get an idea of the number of Durga Pujas celebrated

in the UK, I found on one website that there were over 15 pujas in London alone, and another 20 in the rest of the UK, which is quite impressive. One of the most popular pujas, the Camden Durga Puja in London, was started in 1963. The chief patron of this puja is industrialist Laxmi Niwas Mittal, who hails from Kolkata. This year, a *jatra*, a folk theatre form of Bengal, was performed based on Draupadi's *vastraharan* story in the *Mahabharata*. Popular contemporary singers like Lopamudra Mitra and Joy Sarkar have also performed there.

I heard from some people that another outfit called Prabashi also organises a puja, which is held at Hounslow, near Heathrow, in west London. This year they got a new idol all the way from Kumartuli in Kolkata.

The best part about these Durga Pujas held outside India is that they are not confined to the participation of Bengalis alone. People from different communities also take part. The festive Puja days become fun-filled with cultural activities and desi cuisine. The *bhog* is cooked by the ladies, who also prepare sweets, sold in stalls set up by them.

One thing that is unanimously agreed upon is the preference to spend Durga Puja in London rather than in Kolkata. The reason being the enormous crowds, which make it impossible for people to even have a proper glimpse of the idol in Kolkata, with so much nudging and jostling going around. Here they can enjoy the Pujas in a peaceful and relaxed manner.

Although I was not present during the Pujas in Kolkata this year, I have heard that some puja committees in the city had their themes based around the US and Britain. There were London streets and squares created by artisans in these pandals. But I missed seeing these myself.

In Geneva, the Pujas were held on September 28 and 29 this year. I met quite a few Indians there — 12 families were from Geneva and the others were from Lausanne and Nyon. Durga Puja was started in Switzerland in 1996.

It really touches my heart to see these Indians on foreign soil following their customs and rituals with so much devotion. Although the main *purohit* does the puja, the volunteers do a lot of work to assist the priest. The ladies wearing their saris and men in their kurtas always look impressive, and for a moment, while in the midst of it all, it seems as if I am at a Puja pandal in Kolkata itself.

During my stay in Geneva during the Pujas, I also found several non-Indians present in the puja hall. I met one Ardhendu Ganguly there, who has been actively engaged in the Durga Puja at the centre as a volunteer. He has also been involved with various Indian functions since 1972. The puja was conducted by Swami Amarananda.

As in Bengal or elsewhere, in keeping with Bengalis' love of cultural activities, here too there were functions and musical performances presented by the local Bengali women. After having seen Pujas in Britain and the US, my first Durga Puja in Europe started with Switzerland. In the years to come I hope to see many more outside India.

The Asian Age

November 16, 2017

45

When Gandhi is a Café in Switzerland

Any tourist's dream is to visit Switzerland. When I first went to Switzerland, I realised the reason people wanted to visit this beautiful country. The picture-postcard scenic beauty simply mesmerises the eye. But there is something more interesting than that. That something is the presence of Indian food in this European country.

There are quite a few Indian restaurants in Geneva, even though not too many Indians live there. Among the top restaurants are Rasoi by Vineet, Sajna Restaurant, Little India, Spice of India, India Curry House and Bombay Restaurant, among several others. Then there are a couple of restaurants that immediately drew my attention, like Rajpoute and Jaipur.

Of course, it is not a surprise that one finds a restaurant by the name of Bollywood in Geneva knowing that 'Bollywood' has almost become synonymous with the word 'India'. As if this is not enough, I found another one by the name Restaurant Indian Bollywood. Next time I come here I am sure to find more restaurants with the Bollywood tag!

It is difficult to say which is more popular — Indian food or Bollywood. On the other hand, the tag of Gandhi also helps one to identify an Indian restaurant, so there it was in Geneva — Gandhi café.

Let me start off by talking about Rasoi. Vineet Bhatia, the celebrity chef, has established Rasoi in many parts of the world. The one in Geneva is located on the river Rhone at the Mandarin Oriental Boutique Hotel. The location is terrific as the financial institutions and the upscale shops are all just a stone's throw away. This also happens to be the first fine dining Indian restaurant in Geneva. As is the signature of Vineet, here too he presents traditional Indian food with a modern creative twist.

The restaurant was awarded its first Michelin star in 2009. Being a vegetarian, I have a problem eating everything available on the menu and because of that my choices generally get limited. Here, though, I found a compelling dish — a starter made out of beetroot. Beet is not much used in Indian cooking, so this one called Beet 3 Ways made the menu different. It further explained the dish as Beetroot Potli, Beetroot Momo, Beetroot Galouti and spiced feta *chaat*. Bhel puri of red rice is a must-try.

Spice of India seems to be another favourite of local Indians. The restaurant specialises in North Indian food, specially Punjabi cuisine. But it was the décor that I found more captivating, as it is bright and lively. The colours are so vibrant that a guest entering the place would immediately be prepared for a cuisine that is not only lip-smacking but a feast for the eyes, too.

The one thing I have noticed is that many of the Indian restaurants claim that they serve Asian, Pakistani and Bangladeshi cuisine, which shows that food from this region is popular even in Europe. The entire subcontinent and its flavours seem to have become a source of gastronomical delight.

I tasted some authentic idlis and dosas at a place called Shiva restaurant. This place serves simple and delicious South Indian specialties and is quite popular among the locals.

I was intrigued by the name Gandhi café, so, naturally, I went there. Although the name was Gandhi, it specialised in Punjabi cuisine, especially tandoor. I was taken aback to find that they served non-vegetarian food as well, even though they profess to be inspired by Gandhi. However, I found that this place was quite popular because of its quality. *Aloo gobi, palak paneer* and naan are the favourite dishes as I gathered from those who have visited the place. A variety of pakoras were also available like *gobi, pyaz, aloo, baingan*, paneer, and mixed samosas.

I was quite impressed by the number of vegetarian items on the menu. Apart from a few potato dishes, there was dal, *chana, bharta*, a few paneer-based items, Navratan Korma and vegetable biryani. There were quite a number of rice dishes like lemon rice, *jeera* rice and saffron rice, to name a few. The page that listed naans was interesting as it featured quite a few innovative ones. There was Gandhi Naan — a naan stuffed with vegetables and garlic, Naan Grapes, Coco Naan, Naan Peppers and some others along with *chapati* and *paratha*.

The desserts had gulab jamun, kulfi and something called Gandhi Cup, which was explained as a cup filled with exotic fruits.

Little India on Rue du Prieure was one restaurant that everyone raved about. I decided to try it, and I must say that I was not disappointed. The only regret was, of course, being a vegetarian, I could not eat a lot of things on the menu. There was the usual dal, *aloo* items, *baingan bharta* and two or three paneer items. Raita seems to be everywhere. In the dessert section I found *suji halwa*, which is not usually found in other places.

This place also informed its customers beforehand what

they were going to serve as a special menu for lunch. The entire week's menu was available on the website, allowing people to choose which day to visit according to their food preferences.

So, if you go to Geneva, do not miss out on eating Indian food from one of these restaurants. Though not exactly *ma ke haath ka khana* (a mother's cooking), it is very palatable, and definitely worth tasting.

The Asian Age

December 14, 2017

46

India's National Bird at the UN's Geneva Headquarters

During a recent visit to Geneva, I was pleasantly surprised to find our national bird proudly strutting around the hallowed premises of one of Europe's most iconic buildings — the Palais des Nations. In fact, I never imagined I would spot a peacock in this part of the world! I have only seen them in the wild in Rajasthan or in a few zoos overseas, tagged as India's national bird.

Before I tell you how the Geneva municipality is legally bound to take care of these peacocks, let me share some information about the Palais des Nations, the former headquarters of the League of Nations and the current European headquarters of the United Nations.

I came to Geneva to attend the WFUNA executive committee meeting, which takes place in the landmark United Nations Office at Geneva (UNOG), housed at the Palais des Nations. This humongous complex is located on the prestigious 46-hectare Ariana Park, overlooking Lake Geneva. It was built between 1929 and 1938 to serve as the headquarters for the League of Nations. Over the years, other buildings were added to the complex.

In April 1946, the League of Nations was dissolved at a final assembly held in Geneva. All the assets and properties were handed over to the newly formed United Nations Organisation. The Palais des Nations was one of the prized jewels. It is a symbolic representation of the famous 'spirit of Geneva'.

Geneva has often been hailed as the first international city, and it all started in November 1920, when the citizens of Geneva welcomed delegates from around the world for the first international conference of the League of Nations.

The first time the plan for building this complex was floated, there were some 300 entries received from architects and firms from all over the world. After much deliberation, five were chosen. The huge complex that we see today was added later. The Palais premises have a park, chalets, villas, offices, cafeterias, gardens, halls, a tomb, conference rooms and iconic statues and monuments.

Some of the famous monuments include The Celestial Sphere, The Conquest of Space, The Family, Armillary Sphere, The Great Centaur, The Tower of Loneliness, the cenotaph of Gustave Revilliod, and many more. There is also the famous Human Rights and Alliance of Civilisations Room, from where much of the world's decisions and policies pertaining to human rights are deliberated and executed.

Beneath the Palais des Nations' foundation stone is a 'time capsule', containing a document listing the names of the League of Nations member states, a copy of the covenant of the League and specimen coins of all the countries represented at the League of Nations at the time of its inception.

Each year over one lakh visitors tour the Palais des Nations and 60,000 delegates participate in various conferences. However, about a dozen or so 'special guests' have been permanent members at the Palais des Nations since 1890 by decree. These are peacocks and peahens. I was very surprised to find India's national bird roaming freely on the premises in their splendid colours. Their occasional calls managed to, every now and then, pierce through the stillness of the park.

How did these 'special guests' arrive at the Palais des Nations?

I was curious and made some enquiries. And what I came to know was intriguing. The presence of about a dozen peacocks at the UN headquarters is a legacy of art collector Gustave Revilliod de Rive, who bequeathed his park to the City of Geneva in 1890 based on three conditions — that he be buried at the park after his death, that the peacocks should be allowed to roam freely in the park and that the park should allow access to the masses. All three conditions have been honoured by the city of Geneva. Thus, the peacocks are the 'special guests' of Palais de Nations as per the local law. A cenotaph or tomb of Gustave Revilliod has also been erected within the premises where his mortal remains rest.

For decades, the peafowl have been roaming freely within the premises of Palais des Nations, often seen perching on many of the more than 100-year-old trees planted from all over the world. Most of the peacocks are from the Indian subcontinent. A Japanese zoo had initially gifted some peacocks to the Palais des Nations and the rest were gifted by the Permanent Mission of India in Geneva. The birds are fed and taken care of by the park's gardeners.

Many foreign visitors are surprised at the sight of these magnificent peacocks, which are not native to Switzerland. The visitors can be seen taking selfies and clicking away with their cameras on sighting the peacocks anywhere, even at the entrance of the Assembly Hall! The hefty cost of keeping these feathered guests in style is borne by the United Nations Office at Geneva.

The United Nations Postal Administration office in Palais des Nations came out with a collection of special stamps, which included these peacocks, during its 45th anniversary. Many visitors take a postcard with these stamps on it before posting a goodwill letter home. This has become a popular phenomenon with many visitors.

Ariana Park is also an arboretum with a fantastic collection of over 800 species of trees brought from all over the world. Some 600 species of trees planted here have been labelled with their biological names and countries of origin. All the vegetables grown here are organic.

The park has obtained the coveted Nature Reserve certificate. This certificate is given after several stringent criteria are met. For example, the Palais des Nations never uses hand or mechanised mowers to cut the lush green grass, which grows during springtime. Instead, a flock of sheep is allowed to graze on the grass.

On meeting Michael Moller, the Director-General of the United Nations Office, Geneva, I was gifted with a jar of honey, which was extracted from a beehive housed on the Palais' premises.

Coming back to our national bird, I am glad to find that the peacock has attained a special status in one of Europe's most popular building complexes, visited by people from all over the world. The fact that Geneva is legally bound to honour its promise to retain these birds evokes a sense of pleasant surprise. Thanks to Gustave Revilliod de Rive for ensuring that these birds would be there as long as the Palais des Nations exists.

The Asian Age

May 10, 2018

47

A Jewel in the Taj Crown

I am scheduled to visit the United States on an invitation from Yale University and also due to speak at Princeton University and New York University. Once again, I shall be staying at The Pierre in Manhattan's Upper East Side, which is currently owned by the Taj Group of Hotels or the Tatas. This unique and elegant hotel was started by Frenchman Charles Pierre Casalasco and opened to the public on October 1, 1930, after five years of planning, supported by a group of influential New Yorkers.

In 1940, a part of the property was converted into apartments and has since become the address of the rich and famous. At present, the number of hotel rooms and apartments on each floor are evenly matched.

The Taj Group of Hotels took over the property in 2005. Before that, it was being managed by Four Seasons. The hotel has a manned 24x7 lift, which is a rarity in New York. It boasts the largest banquet hall in NYC. After staying at The Pierre over the years, I am convinced that this hotel has the best housekeeping services in the world and is one of the best-run establishments. The meticulous attention to detail in housekeeping is worth mentioning and can't skip the regular traveller's eyes.

The Pierre has been the centre of attraction for Hollywood stars for generations. The last time I put up at The Pierre, I had met Karambir Singh Kang, area director for the US, who was the general manager of Taj Mumbai during the 26/11 terror attacks of 2008. Karambir had taken me around The Pierre Hall of Fame Museum, then commemorating 90 years of its completion. Besides the grandeur, glory and history, the museum also reflects the inimitable 'Tajness' of the place.

While glamour, romance, history, fame and innovation have always been a part and parcel of The Pierre, the hotel has continuously transformed itself under different owners. Moving from the café society of the late 1930s and 1940s to ushering in big band entertainment during the ownership of oil tycoon John Paul Getty. And from there, seamlessly blending into the jet-set age that replaced the café society culture and introduced supper clubs through its famous Cotillion Room.

In 1959, Paul Getty sold over 70 cooperative apartments in the building to private owners. This practice continues till date. Among the permanent fixtures at The Pierre are

Elizabeth Taylor, Greek shipping tycoon Aristotle Onassis, Viacom Entertainment company chairman Summer Redstone, Mohamed Al-Fayed of Harrods and others. The famous patrons of the hotel include Coco Charles, Henry Fonda, Aristotle Onassis, John Paul Getty, Pierre Cardin, Mohamed Al-Fayed and so on.

By 1956, The Pierre had become the centre of Hollywood in New York. Audrey Hepburn was a regular. A ceremony to celebrate her Oscar win for *Roman Holiday* was held in the hotel in 1954. Elizabeth Taylor married Eddie Fisher and bought an apartment at The Pierre in 1959.

In the 1960s, The Pierre Grill, with an open kitchen, was introduced, where Indian curries were served by the tableside. Other innovations included Birdcage — a glass cocktail bar that was hung from the ceiling of The Rotunda — a large ballroom.

In 1967, Peter Dowling, who owned The Carlyle, took over The Pierre. Much of the classic look and elegance of the hotel can be traced to him. By the time the Beatles arrived in the United States, big bands and supper clubs were passé. The Pierre adapted again and opened a nightclub called Artefacts at The Pierre Hall of Fame. The Cotillion and the Roof Garden Terrace were transformed into ballrooms.

Fashion superstars took over the hotel in the 1970s.

Rudolph Valentino made The Pierre the centre of the fashion world in New York. Cher, Andy Warhol, Liza Minnelli, Yves Saint Laurent, Hubert de Givenchy, Barbra Streisand and others all became regulars. The ballroom and the entertainment spaces of The Pierre have remained the premier venues for corporate functions, galas, social events, fundraisers and weddings ever since.

Isidor Sharp, the founder of Four Seasons Hotels, bought The Pierre in 1980. Years later, in 2005, identifying The Pierre as an ideal property to enter the North American market, Ratan Tata bought the hotel and made it a part of his prestigious collection of Taj Hotels, Resorts, Palaces and Safaris, a subsidiary of the Tata conglomerate.

Over time, some major renovations have taken place, including the restoration of The Rotunda alongside Perrine, the latest restaurant to open. The Rotunda was hand painted by renowned American artist Edward Melcarth in 1967.

The Pierre lobby now reflects the Taj Group's rich Indian heritage. A century-old handwoven paisley pashmina shawl by G.R. Santosh is one such signature piece of art. The Pierre's Rajput Suite is inspired by India's artistic traditions, including hand-carved furnishing and bronze statues of Indian deities. The hotel also has a Tata Presidential Suite.

Many works of local contemporary artists have found a place at the Perrine French-American restaurant. Each day, Perrine features a classic dish from The Pierre's vintage menu dating back to the 1930s.

Many famous films, including *Volcano, Scent of a Woman, Trainwreck* and *Ocean's 8,* have been shot in this hotel. The 160-metre tall hotel has 189 rooms, of which 49 are suites. Eleven of these suites are categorised as Grand Suites. The New York City Landmarks Preservation Commission designated The Pierre as a historic landmark in 1981.

Another novelty of the hotel is that it offers all its guests a free drop-off service to anywhere in Manhattan on a first-come-first-served basis in a Tata Jaguar. Additionally, if you are staying here, don't forget to grab a bite of its fabled *aloo paratha*, which is perhaps the best in New York.

The Asian Age

March 16, 2020

Social Issues

Dedicated to

All the ***Editors*** *who have supported me and published my columns despite many challenges and opposition*

I always wondered why somebody doesn't do something about that. Then I realized I was somebody.

— Lily Tomlin

48

Chasing Status

I got a call from my industrialist friend from South India seeking a favour. He wanted me to recommend his friend as an Honorary Consul of any country in Kolkata. Further, my friend requested me to leverage my diplomatic contacts in Delhi and arrange for him to meet some of the Ambassadors who could be instrumental in appointing this friend as their Honorary Consul.

Becoming an Honorary Consul is a status symbol among industrialists in Kolkata and may be elsewhere too. In the past five years, the number of Honorary Consuls in our city has increased rapidly.

It is perceived to be a ticket to a charmed circle and a gateway to round-the-year parties in star hotels, where you get to meet and rub shoulders with the high and the mighty and the glitterati. Basically, Honorary Consuls are akin to the trader representatives or those who articulate or facilitate trading interests of their respective countries in designated areas.

There was a time when very few were appointed Consul Generals and were delegated with the power to issue visas. Initially, countries used to appoint only those with whom they had strong business connections.

But over the last few years, this criterion has been done away with. In some cases, a person who just happened to visit that country for the first time ended up becoming its Honorary Consul. In other cases, it has become a family affair, with the post of Honorary Consul being passed on to another member of the same family. These days the post of Honorary Consul is being chased as a status symbol.

For the nouveau riche industrialists in the city, this is an easy way to mingle with bureaucrats, diplomats and celebs, and get invited to high-profile government events.

The trade-off for taking care of the logistics for the Ambassadors and visitors of the country they represent is hardly much when compared to what they are out to seek and leverage in the name of being an Honorary Consul. It is, however, unfair to paint all Honorary Consuls with a tainted brush. There are Honorary Consuls who have added a lot of respect and understanding towards the country they represent in Kolkata. But they are rare and are seldom seen in these weekly receptions or parties, nor do they have a need to be recognised by this article.

In the last seven years, I have been approached by the

representatives of three different countries with proposals to become their Honorary Consul in Kolkata. I have declined their offer because I have strong reservations in putting up the national flag of another country on my car, office or residence. However, one of the Honorary Consul's offices in Kolkata did extend to me a position on paper and issued an airport permanent entry card that gave me access to certain restricted areas.

With due respect to all my friends who are Honorary Consuls, I am not at all comfortable being an Indian citizen and representing some other country. Many a time I have had arguments on this issue with my well-wishers and friends.

What can the tag of an Honorary Consul bring other than the guilt of representing some other nation in my own country?

At the end of the day, however, it is a matter of personal choice. But there is little room for doubt that the office of the Honorary Consul is gradually being demeaned.

Cityscape, Hindustan Times, Kolkata

July 12, 2010

49

RSVP — What's That?

I recently hosted a small get-together for Sharmila Tagore, who was in the city for a day. Though it was well-attended, I was expecting some more invitees since I had received no regret notes from their end. But then, do people in Kolkata give any importance to 'RSVP'?

Last month, I was at a friend's for lunch. The small gathering had a mix of politicians, bureaucrats, artists, industrialists and diplomats and their better halves. After starters and mocktails, we approached the main course on an elaborately laid dining table, with nametags marking the seating order. Just then, a couple arrived. The hosts rushed into hasty action, trying to accommodate them on the table, and apologised, saying that since they had received no confirmation, they presumed the couple would not be able to join them. The couple merely said they hadn't seen the details on the invite.

In Kolkata, it is fashionable to *not* be on time. Whatever time an invite may mention, many guests do not arrive before 9pm, and then say they have to rush somewhere else, and so on. That is why many party invitations clearly mention the duration of the function or reception.

The French phrase *'Répondez, s'il vous plait'* (RSVP), meaning 'please respond', is freely used on invites across India, but the overwhelming majority of guests and hosts do not know what it means. The person inviting you would like you to say whether you accept the invitation. In the West, etiquette demands that if you receive a formal, written invitation, you should reply promptly.

For hosts who plan a dinner party, a wedding, or a reception, this is important from a practical point of view, because they need to know how much food and drink to provide.

Most invitations carry a 'regrets only' note, meaning that the hosts will count on your presence, unless told otherwise.

I have organised various functions, dinners and get-togethers, from Chetla *basti*, to pockets in Burrabazar, to star hotels. I can't recall a single occasion when a fair number of invitees bothered to confirm their presence.

Even for programmes involving protocol, RSVP is not given the importance it merits. Often, when you call celebrities and politicians, they don't even acknowledge having received an invite. I see no reason for not responding with a line or an SMS.

I have seen VVIPs come in late for functions, putting the organisers in an awkward situation as they offend somebody with a request to vacate their first-row seat for the latecomers. This can cause problems ranging from embarrassment to a huge waste of resources.

At many house parties, I have had to change seating orders or even set up a buffet at the last minute because some invitees informed us at the eleventh hour that they would join us late.

We often blame the traffic for being late but are there any excuses for not responding to RSVPs?

Cityscape, Hindustan Times, Kolkata

September 5, 2010

50

The Devil is in the Detail

Last weekend, I flew into Kolkata from Delhi to host a dinner for Gulzar *saab* at ITC Sonar. On my way to the Delhi airport, I picked up books by Gulzar for the guests at the dinner, losing my credit card in the process.

However, talking of airports and credit cards, I remember an email from a gentleman who wrote about a bitter experience with the Standard Chartered Bank Privilege Card. He was holding a SCB Titanium Card, on a free-for-lifetime scheme, and was offered a Platinum Card by the bank at an annual charge of Rs 6,000, plus taxes, along with a Priority Pass that entitled him to use the domestic airport lounges free of cost, and a USD 27 charge for using international airport lounges.

As a frequent traveller, he accepted the card, and used it at the Delhi and Kolkata lounges after confirming that no charges were payable. To his surprise, he soon received a bill of USD 27, plus taxes. Naturally, he felt the bank had sold him the card on false pretences.

True, perhaps. But I think the gentleman may have missed the fine print, which is so small that is almost impossible to read with the naked eye. So, most of us skip it.

I have often wondered at the rationale of printing terms and conditions relating to transactions in a size barely visible to the eye. These disclaimers pertaining to every agreement, purchase, sale, investment or contract are a very important aspect of any transaction. They merit proper understanding and should actually be in large, legible print so that no one can miss them.

The history of fine print stems from the concept of caveat emptor, which means, "Let the buyer be aware". But I have never come across a disclaimer that is legible. They are always, as the name suggests, in "fine", or very small print. The intention seems to be to discourage the buyer from reading it, while going by the rule book to ensure statutory compliance.

When we invest without reading the fine print, it means we accept something without being aware of what to do if the product is not up to the mark. Disclaimers hold investors solely responsible for all contractual deeds and actions. One can imagine the seriousness of this issue while dealing with medical products, investments and other services that may involve one's life's earnings.

Since most of us fail to read the footnote, we unknowingly place the other party on higher ground, to dictate terms once the product is sold.

Imagine the fate of students who rush to enrol in various courses without reading the fine print, to later find that the courses do not have the affiliations necessary to get a job.

Sometimes, the fine print has a clause that says, "Rules are liable to change without notice".

If we can't read such important points, we end up on the weaker side of the law, if not on the wrong side, in case of a dispute.

Many companies insert a caveat, spoken very rapidly, in audio-visual commercials. One gets the feeling the company has something to hide but is compelled by the law to reveal it. So, why not a verbal vomit which few understand?

The devil, indeed, is in the details.

Cityscape, Hindustan Times, Kolkata

February 20, 2011

51

Double Standards

Top international luxury brands have a halo effect that inspires awe and envy among Indians. The thrifty Indians' lust for luxe has drawn scores of big names to set up shop here and reap the dividends of their shopping safaris.

But all is not well. Let me share my not-so-pleasant recent experience with three reputable multinational brands in India that have led me to the question: Do these brands treat Indian customers at par with those in the West?

The first incident took place in Delhi in June when I picked up a L'Occitane en Provence soap. When I opened the packet, I found the soap was totally dry. I thought the dry Indian weather was the culprit. On my second visit to the shop, I asked the staff member in L'Occitane uniform if they were selling old products. He said, no way. I emptied a basket full of soaps in front of him and checked the expiry dates. About half the bars had expired about a month or two ago but were still on sale. The shopkeeper feigned surprise and gave me the usual blarney that this was the first time this had happened.

On my return to Kolkata, I wrote a mail about my experience to the London head office of Customer Service, MELVITA UK, L'Occitane Ltd., Beauty Products. No reply. After two weeks, I forwarded the same message to them.

This time, within 15 minutes, I received a call from the Indian agent, who once again threw up a flurry of excuses — how he had tried to get in touch with me in vain during the past two weeks and so on.

I did not argue. I was sure he hadn't acted on the first email and was calling me for the first time. He offered me a box of soap bars free of charge. He said he could courier it to me or I could collect it from the South City showroom in Kolkata. I refused.

Last month, I was at the Dunhill UB City Mall in Bangalore. I saw a leather bag, and out of curiosity, asked the price. A week earlier, I had picked up the same bag at a 50 percent discount from the Dunhill Emporium Mall, Delhi. On being told the price, I asked if there was a discount. The sales staff said, "Dunhill never offers a discount on any leather bags at any of its showrooms." I did not stretch the conversation because I already had a somewhat odd experience when I bought the bag in Delhi.

The lady at the Delhi showroom had showed me a

pair of sunglasses, saying there were only 250 such in the world and this was the only one in India. But when I checked, the same sunglasses were available in another Dunhill showroom in India. When I reported this incident to the head in Mumbai, he apologised on behalf of both the store managers.

The last incident happened last week in Kolkata. I had sent my Bose music system to their service centre in Santiniketan Building for servicing. My man said the staff had said it would take 10 days to check if the system was OK. When I called the service centre, a lady told me, "Sir, for three-and-half months we have had no engineers."

A global brand like Bose doesn't have an engineer for over three months? Is it just because this is India that one can get away with anything? Can a company like Bose afford to have a similar situation in Paris, London, New York or any other leading cities in the West?

Surely it would blow craters in their reputation.

Such service from renowned global brands in three different cities of India makes me wonder if these brands are being let down by their local partners. Or is it some kind of consumer apartheid when it comes to servicing Indian clients?

Cityscape, Hindustan Times, Kolkata

September 11, 2011

52

What's in a Name? A Lot!

From Québec province, Canada. This province, three times the size of France, is perhaps the only Francophone region in the North American continent. The predominantly French-speaking population and the resource-rich region's seasons are as distinct as its culture and language — mild spring, hot summer, colourful chilly autumn and a freezing, white winter.

Another unique feature of Québec is that it is one of the few regions in the world where women, by law, can keep their maiden name after marriage. I wonder why so-called "progressive" countries, which advocate gender equality, are such laggards when it comes to implementing a law that enables women to retain their maiden name after marriage.

Why change your surname, given to you by birth, just for the sake of marriage? Why is an important institution like marriage so biased against one gender?

The story of equal rights should begin with mutual

respect. Changing somebody's surname amounts to disrespecting that person. How would men feel if their names were changed?

For the sake of identity, it may be optional for a woman to use her husband's name, but only if she wishes to. This is where Québec comes in. Until 1981, women in Québec would traditionally adopt their husband's surnames, but their maiden names remained their legal name.

All this changed after the passage of a 1981 provincial law to promote gender equality as outlined in the Québec Charter of Rights, which ordained that no change may be made to a person's name without the authorisation of the registrar of civil status or of the court.

Women wishing to change their names upon marriage must, therefore, go through the same procedure as those changing their names for other reasons. Only the registrar of civil status may authorise a name change, and for specific reasons.

For example, the name a person uses may not correspond to that on the birth certificate; the name may be of foreign origin or too difficult to pronounce or write in its original form or; it may invite ridicule or have become infamous. Marriage is not even listed among the reasons for a change. But a woman may use her husband's name socially, and eventually apply to change it under the 'general use' clause.

In India, a woman usually adopts her husband's family name after marriage, and in some orthodox families, may even have to change her full name. Notable exceptions are matrilineal societies, such as the Nairs of Kerala, where women retain their maiden names after marriage, and the children take her name, rather than their father's.

Ditto Meghalaya, where it is common for women not to change their names after marriage. The first name is the one parents choose for their child, and the last name is, by default, the mother's.

Many Indian laws are antiquated and in conflict with the spirit of gender equality. It is high time India should do what Québec did in 1981, change the law and give a little more respect to women.

Cityscape, Hindustan Times, Kolkata

October 30, 2011

53

A Big Fat Kolkata Wedding

I normally don't like attending weddings. But recently, I was back in Mumbai after almost 17 years to do just that — attend a wedding, that of Calcutta-based industrialist Ghanshyam Sarda's daughter Prerna with Abhinav Jhunjhunwala, son of Amitabh Jhunjhunwala, vice chairman and director, Reliance Anil Dhirubhai Ambani Group (ADAG).

I attended the pre-wedding *sangeet* function on Friday (January 27) in the ballroom of Taj Mahal Palace in Colaba. The ballroom was teeming with people, far more than it could accommodate comfortably. The leading industrialists of the country had turned up in full strength at the bash hosted by the Jhunjhunwalas.

The scene at the Taj Lands End on Saturday (January 28) was straight out of a Bollywood film. By 4pm, the lane leading to the hotel was chock-a-block with cars. A red carpet from the road went all the way into the hotel.

The arrival of the Jhunjhunwala *baraat* embodied what

the world knows as the 'big fat Indian wedding'. People thronged both sides of the road as the bridegroom's entourage made a gala entry led by industrialist Anil Ambani. Celebrity guests, including Aamir Khan and his wife, producer Kiran Rao, were among a host of other high-profile names.

I stood there on the other side of the door with a group who had come down from Kolkata in full strength to welcome the bridegroom. Aamir and Kiran were in the middle of the *baraat*. I also spotted Prasoon Joshi in the midst of it all, whom I had recently met at Jaipur Literature Festival.

As the evening stretched into night — on the hotel poolside lawn that wore an exquisite new look — the seemingly endless show of glamour and opulence went on and on and on, as did the roll call of the rich and famous, with all the expected razzmatazz.

Shah Rukh Khan, the Bachchans, Vidhu Vinod Chopra, Karan Johar, Madhur Bhandarkar, Rakesh Jhunjhunwala, Smriti Irani, Prakash Jha, Farhan Akhtar and so on. Everybody present was somebody.

Aamir Khan made the evening extra special for many guests from Kolkata by posing with them for photos during the *pheras*. SRK, who arrived post-9.30pm, greeted the parents of the bride and groom with his trademark charm.

There was a touch of Kolkata everywhere. From Sabyasachi (Mukherjee) saris to the different types of *sandesh* at dinner to the traditional marriage songs on loop that are a must in all Marwari weddings in Kolkata. Then there was the Russell Street *phuchkawala* and Kolkata's famous *jhal muri* during the high tea that was lapped up by Aamir, who launched into a non-stop *phuchka* feast!

There are many high-voltage Indian weddings where money flows like water. But I would remember this one for its sheer elegance, its hospitality, its personal touch and the attention given to the smallest details, including the incorporation of all things Kolkata.

Utsav Parekh was making sure that every guest had eaten well. It reminded me of Utsav's son's wedding at ITC Sonar in Kolkata when Ghanshyam Sarda was receiving guests at the entrance. This is what friendship is all about.

For all those Kolkattans who attended, this was a memorable wedding — from being welcomed by Tina Ambani at the reception to having Anil Ambani attending to the food arrangements to the warmth of the bride's and groom's families, who made everyone feel like a Bachchan or an Ambani.

The Telegraph-t2, Kolkata

February 6, 2012

54

The Great Indian Tradition of Naming and Renaming

'A rose by any other name would smell as sweet' is a commonly quoted line from William Shakespeare's play, *Romeo and Juliet*, in which Juliet argues that the names of things do not matter, only what things are.

In India, however, particularly in Rajasthan, the *naamkaran* (name-giving) ceremony of a child is an important aspect of life and tradition. This ceremony is performed either on the 11th or on the 101st day after the child's birth. Often, it is an elaborate social ceremony with a family priest reciting mantras from the Vedas and blessing the child in the presence of womenfolk from the locality, who assemble to sing songs and offer their good wishes to the child.

During the last winter season, I was on a merry-go-round trip across London, Kolkata, Jaipur, New Delhi and Bengaluru, both working and attending events, wedding ceremonies/receptions in all these cities. I came across a few wedding cards where I found that the girl's name was followed by another name in brackets. I had seen such cards earlier, too; these reminded me of a recent incident.

A few weekends back, while I was in Bengaluru, I called up a friend who had got married a couple of years ago and had shifted to that city recently. She sent me an SMS asking me to contact her on her landline as the mobile network reception in her area was poor.

But when I called on the landline and asked for her, a maid who answered the phone said it was a wrong number. I re-dialled and asked for the lady by her name, and again got the same answer. I checked my cell phone once again and thought there must have been some mistake and I had ended up with a wrong number. I emailed her asking for her landline number. The next day, she called me on my mobile from the same 'wrong number' that I had dialled just a day back.

But why did the maid say there was nobody by that name living in that house?

That is a story in itself. The maid had said so because the in-laws of my friend had changed her name after marriage. As the maid had no idea what her earlier name was, she was right in her own way. And the reason why the lady's in-laws had changed her name after marriage was because her husband's grandmother, who is no more, had had the same name.

This really comes as no surprise to me. I don't know about other communities, but in the one that I belong to, it is common practice to change a girl's name after marriage, if it matches that of any of the family members, past or present, and the new name is mentioned in the wedding cards as well. Look closely at these cards — you will sometimes find the bride's name is followed by another one in brackets.

I find this very strange. How can someone's name, which has been given at birth, be changed like this in a jiffy just because someone in the family she is marrying into happens to have the same name? The supposed logic for this is that if the newly-wed bride is called by her name, it would mean disrespecting the elderly woman in the family with the same name — an aunt, mother-in-law or grandmother, even a great-grandmother. Even if the groom's sister has the same name, the bride's name is changed. One question: why not change the daughter's name instead?

One of the biggest underlying lies in our society is the concept *bahu beti ek samaan* (that a daughter-in-law and a daughter are equal). That is never the case. The fact is that a daughter-in-law can never be truly regarded as a daughter. I have often wondered what if the name of the boy or bridegroom happens to be the same as that of anyone in the family he is marrying into? Is there any need for him to change his name? I think not. Men are not expected to do this, and this 'rule' applies only to women.

It is fairly common for a girl to change her surname after marriage but changing her first name altogether just because there's another member of her new family with the same name is really bizarre! It also goes against the very spirit of *naamkaran* — when a name is chosen and mantras recited to solemnise the occasion. Another fact is that some families, while renaming a bride, consult an astrologer to pick a 'suitable' name.

Why take so much trouble to name a girl child when very often, later in life, this very name can be changed in a jiffy just because someone else had the same name in the family she is marrying into?

A name is something very personal and sticks to us like a label. If one day a close friend or relative with whom I have grown up is suddenly given a new name, I am sure to have a lot of difficulty getting used to that new name. Imagine how much difficulty that person may have in responding to a new name. It all seems so unfair.

Meanwhile, The Asian Age

March 1, 2012

55

Rituals that Linger

The government has decided to pull down the curtains on the 160-year old telegram service in India from mid-July 2013. This once invaluable service in our era of SMS and email has outlived its utility. That is often the story with technology, which gets obsolete every now and then in the wake of new inventions.

There is a similar parallel between technology and rituals i.e., both may become obsolete. However, one glaring difference is that rituals, howsoever obsolete, have a tendency to linger, while technologies fall by the wayside. To put things in perspective, let me relate a recent incident.

A few days ago, I got a Brahmin *dakshina* card by post from someone known to me. His grandfather had expired at the age of over 85, which I knew of. It was a very simple bereavement card with a black border and black ink printed on a white card requesting me (recipient) to donate the amount of money enclosed with the card to my family Brahmin priest.

But I was surprised to find that the envelope, supposed to have the money, was empty. Not only that, there was a fresh staple mark, which indicated that someone had taken the money out and re-stapled the envelope, possibly in transit. It was nothing new, as it had happened a number of times before. But I also observed that these cards with money seem to be decreasing year after year.

But still the number of such Brahmin *dakshina* cards sent by post or courier each year runs into lakhs and presumably the losses too are staggering. This is a very common traditional bereavement ritual aimed at soliciting the support of different Brahmin priests to pray for the departed soul.

Traditionally, following a death in the family, the card used to be sent requesting the recipients to send their Brahmin priest to collect the *dakshina* in person. Times have changed and it is not always possible for the Brahmins to collect the money, which generally used to be a paltry sum of Rs 11 or 21. Also, not all families have such traditional Brahmins. In fact, many times I get envelopes containing Rs 5. However, the fact of the matter is that the entire purpose is defeated since the money never reaches the recipient at times. As far as Grade A couriers are concerned, it costs more than the money itself being sent, and if one declares that the envelope has money in it, the couriers, as far as my knowledge goes, wouldn't even accept it.

With due respect to the sentiments of the senders, I think they should think seriously and take a call on whether they should at all continue with this tradition or do away with it just as the government is planning to phase out the telegram services in India, which has served its purpose and is no longer relevant in this era of fast communication.

Cityscape, Hindustan Times, Kolkata
June 23, 2013

56

Disaster Relief or Total Disaster?

I have been coordinating with different NGOs supporting relief for the 'Himalayan tsunami' in Uttarakhand. As the unofficial death toll mounted, evacuating thousands of stranded pilgrims across vast stretches of mountainous terrain was the principal administrative concern as much as providing basic amenities like food, water, medical help and shelter.

As bodies floated down rivers and survivors brought home tales of horror, the fate of thousands remained unknown to their dear ones. The Uttarakhand government's good intentions fell far short when it came to their ability to conduct relief work, and all hopes were pinned on the Army and Air Force that set out to fight yet another enemy — the inclement weather — to save thousands of lives.

Civil society outfits, welfare organisations and NGOs have come forward to support the government efforts, but the slow and tepid reaction of private corporate houses to come forward with funds and resources has been noticeable. Could it be that private companies had given funds and support without public fanfare? My sources, however, tell me this isn't so.

The number of visitors to the Kedarnath shrine have increased from one lakh in 1998 to nearly six lakhs in 2012. A spate of mindless hydro-power projects and rampant deforestation and violation of ecological norms has exacerbated the calamity, making it a man-made disaster, according to many environmental experts.

I was horrified to discover how, in this crisis, disaster management was a disaster in itself.

There has been an utter lack of coordination and planning, with no cohesive strategy, among various organisations in providing relief. Also, another fact that has come to the fore is that our large private sector companies seem to have a small heart when it comes to giving back to society.

But the most glaring omission was the lack of coordination among NGOs and social welfare organisations, which made much of the relief effort meaningless. The result: a colossal wastage of money and resources at such a critical juncture because of sheer mismanagement and a mindless approach. There were also some omissions due to lack of experience, foresight and oversight. For example, there were several trucks of rice and wheat flour that had come in by way of donations, but there wasn't a single kilo of lentils, pulses or vegetables. There was no synergy between the material needed and the materials made available.

The situation can be explained further by the fact that there were food provisions and match boxes, but no oil or fuel. Of what use would these relief materials have been even if these had reached the starving pilgrims stranded in the remote mountainous terrain? Is it possible to cook food without fuel?

There was an urgent need for paediatrics and medicines, but instead there were packets full of painkillers.

Likewise, many vital links in the support chain were missing, thus derailing the entire effort. In some cases, the social groups, instead of coordinating, seemed to compete with each other for photo opportunities.

Also, nobody asked who is going to receive these trucks. Except for a few leading NGOs, the entire relief material was dependent on transporters in order to be delivered.

India probably has the world's oldest disaster relief code, which started in 1880. The Great Famine of 1876-1878 had led to the constitution of the first Famine Commission of 1880. This relief code provides details of the relief to be given by the government to the affected people. In spite of such a long history of relief work, India hasn't moved on much, or else how does one explain the chaos during the Uttarakhand relief operations?

It also dawned on me how correct Uttarakhand Chief Minister Vijay Bahuguna was when he said, "Give us what we want and when we want, instead of just sending truckloads of materials."

Unlike the private sector giants, the 'Maharatnas' and the 'Navratnas' of the public sector were more forthcoming in contributing funds and resources towards relief. As of now, Kolkata-based Coal India Ltd. has made possibly the largest single contribution of Rs 25 crore towards relief.

My initial SMS appeal to many individuals and leading industrialists to support the cause in whatever way possible drew responses mostly from small and medium businessmen and traders, hardly any from Grade-A industrialists or corporate groups. The old reasoning that they prefer to do their bit silently, without fanfare, seems to be more like an excuse.

I think it is time private corporations should come to the forefront and declare what they are contributing in support of this national disaster. Civil-society is definitely keen to know who does what for the cause. After all, some of these leading private companies are also some of the biggest beneficiaries of projects undertaken in the Himalayas.

It may also be time for the government to introduce a national disaster tax separately on the so-called 'billionaires' club'. Perhaps, a special tax could be levied on top private sector firms to create a corpus to be used in unprecedented national-level disasters and calamities like this one.

There is so much to be learned from American billionaires and individuals like Warren Buffet, Larry Ellison, Bill and Melinda Gates, George Soros, Howard Hughes and others, who have made philanthropy one of their major long-term goals, contributing generously and effectively.

On June 27, a newspaper quoted Bill Gates as saying, "I am sure that philanthropy in India will continue to grow... as people are interested in philanthropy." How I wish his words would come true!

Contributions, however, should not always be measured in terms of money. In some cases, valuable contributions have been made by entities like Google, even though they were physically nowhere close to the disaster site. A small move on Google's part to introduce a search field — 'resources related to Uttarakhand Floods' — was of immense help to those who wanted to post or seek information about their loved ones, those had left home for the Himalayan shrines and were still missing or untraceable.

Focus, The Asian Age

July 9, 2013

57

Here's Some Feedback on the Feedback Form

For a number of years now, I have been staying at various five-star hotels at home and abroad, including some of the biggest hotel chains in the world. I have observed various things that have aroused my curiosity and I have also written about them.

I have noticed something in five-star properties, which may seem trivial from the guests' point of view but can actually make or break careers. This is common to all the top hotels the world over.

The issue at hand is that in their endeavour to serve the customer better, hotel chains have the practice of giving customer feedback cards with the food ordered via room service. This feedback card is separate from the overall feedback form which the hotel gives its guests while checking out or the email version sent to them later.

This 2x3 inch card, which comes with the food trolley,

seeks the patron's feedback on the quality of service, order delivery, efficiency and also on presentation, quality and the taste of the food served. The end-user can exercise their options in 'Yes' or 'No' regarding the service. The card, often on the front fold, mentions 'You are being served by' and there is a space for the name of the bearer or butler who takes the food trolley to the room.

The very purpose of this feedback card is to raise the standard of service and also to understand the needs of the patrons. But there is much more than what meets the eye. Many hotels link this feedback form response to rate the efficiency of the employee concerned.

But what I have noticed in many hotels is that the feedback card does not mention the name of the person serving the food. This has many ramifications. The first time I noticed this, I had doubts about this whole exercise being a serious one. How can a hotel assess its staff if the name of the person serving a guest is not mentioned anywhere in the feedback form? I find it a little odd for a guest to ask for the name of the butler serving the food and writing it on the form.

Very often the staff members serving the guests are trainees. This is mentioned on their badge. How will hotels assess a particular staffer whose name does not feature anywhere? The absence of a name scores out the element of seriousness in the feedback card. After all, what is a feedback card for the guest is also a service assessment card for the hotel. Rating the efficiency of a staffer is linked to points earned and accumulated on the basis of the feedback. Many hotels have this. It has a direct bearing on the career of the staffer. It could be rewarding or could be the end of the road.

I think filling in a nameless card is a meaningless exercise. After all, "quality of food and service" is one of the most critical areas in the highly competitive hospitality sector. The guests who check into hotels should also take this seriously and should, in their own interest, spare a minute to respond to the feedback forms, which, I feel, are valuable inputs that can actually help hotels raise the standards of service. I have been quite amazed by the alacrity of the response from certain brands to the queries and issues that I have raised in the past. I hope the next time I order food from room service, the feedback card has a name on it.

Cityscape, Hindustan Times, Kolkata

September 8, 2013

58

Divided in Birth and in Death

Last week, I was in Churu, Rajasthan, the village where I was born. The reason for my sudden visit was a funeral that I had to attend at the local burning ghat or crematorium, where two things really caught my attention.

I noticed that there were a few very beautiful old structures, which are called *chhatris* in the local language. Inside these structures, there were stone plates fixed on the walls on which prices of gold, silver and food grains etc., were engraved according to the prevailing rates at the time when they were built and the day the stone plaques were fixed.

Muslim workers or artisans had built most of these stone plates. It is evident from their names written under those plates with Lord Ganesha's name on top. It was a pleasant thing to know that a strong communal harmony existed between the Hindus and Muslims.

After talking to a few people, I was in for a surprise yet again, when I came to know that there were about six to seven different caste-specific burning ghats, meant for different Hindu castes, in the same area, including those for 'lower' castes. In fact, in all, there were more than 15 burning ghats in town.

The so-called 'lower' castes have separate burning ghats for Darji, Taknail, Meghwal and Gurjar communities. There is one burning ghat common for Malli, Khatti and Kumhar castes. There is a separate one for the Oswal community and also a separate burning ghat for Jain monks. In fact, a few families like the Khemkas, Baglas and Mantris have their personal burning ghats, which is for their family members only.

My surprise gave way to a realisation that the caste system still divides people, even after death. On returning to Jaipur, when I asked someone, to my utter surprise, I was informed that in a city like Jaipur, too, there are a few burning ghats on the basis of caste. For example, the Pink City's Chandpole cremation ground — the oldest and the biggest — has separate areas assigned for different castes.

So, there is no point blaming the small-town mindset when the situation in the capital of one of India's largest states is no different.

Rajasthanis form ethno-linguistic groups that are distinct in their language, history, cultural and religious practices, social structure, literature, and art. However, there are many different castes and communities, with diversified traditions of their own.

Major sub-ethnic groups are Ahir, Jat, Gurjar, Rajput, Mali, Meena, Bhil, Kalvi, Garasia, Kanjar and so on. I can understand different rituals and last rites for Hindus, Muslims and Christians, but such segregation on the basis of caste within Hinduism for obsequies seemed quite disquieting. It's like we stand divided in birth as well as in death.

Recently, I read a media report that said the Urban Improvement Trust (UIT) of Jaisalmer, in a recent meeting, decided to please the various communities — from smaller ones like *darzi* and *kumhar* to brahmin sub-groups, by resolving to construct separate cremation grounds for 47 caste and communities.

Accordingly, the UIT issued tender notices in local newspapers for the project that is estimated to cost Rs 5 crore.

I wonder are we really progressing by clinging to old and divisive traditions that create apartheid among the dead? It's something we should have done away with a long time back.

Cityscape, Hindustan Times, Kolkata

September 29, 2013

59

Tiger, Tiger Running Out?

According to the National Tiger Conservation Authority, at the turn of the 20th century, India was home to some 40,000 tigers. Today, their number in the wild does not exceed 4,000. This story echoes that of other animals, such as the one-horned rhinoceros, whose population has declined to fewer than 2,400 in India.

The fate of some domesticated species is equally worrisome. For example, the camel population has decreased from 600,000 to 250,000 in the past few decades due to wanton slaughter for meat. The situation is akin to a 'silent holocaust', which, continuing at the same pace, will leave India with no more than 10,000 camels.

Tigers, rhinos, camels and other animals are facing the threat of extinction in India. But for a gargantuan governmental effort, tigers, in particular, would have vanished long ago.

I have been an animal lover since childhood, and it was only natural for me as an adult to become a wildlife activist. Tigers have fascinated me all of my life and my crowning glory as a tiger lover arrived in August 2013, when I bid for, and adopted, a young yet-to-be-named Royal Bengal tigress at the Alipore Zoological Garden in Kolkata, the capital of the eastern Indian state of West Bengal, and home to the world's second largest species of the big cats.

What began as a hobby, over the years, evolved into a matter of grave concern for the very existence of these animals. No informed wildlife preservationist in India can rest in peace in the wake of media reports and troubling statistics that allude to an enormous conservation task at hand. I am no exception.

In September 2013, I learned from the news that one of the largest and strongest networks of poachers in India had been busted with the arrest of a notorious 65-year-old tiger parts trader, Surajpal, alias Chacha, who, along with his nephew Sarju, is said to have killed 300 tigers in the past 30 years in order to smuggle hides, bones and skulls out of the country, particularly to China, making millions of dollars in the process.

This revelation was an eye-opener. While I was always aware of a poaching problem in India, like many others, I had no idea of the enormity of the crisis. Police recovered 18 kilograms of tiger bones, nails and skulls at Surajpal's, who ran his operations from Delhi. The authorities also confiscated 50 million Indian rupees in cash (approximately US $100,000).

The Central Bureau of Investigation (CBI), the top investigative agency in India, and the Wildlife Crime Control Bureau had been searching for Chacha since 2005, when they learnt about his activities with the arrest of another infamous poacher, Sansar Chand Gujjar, who is said to have traded in several animal parts, having killed over 250 tigers, 2,000 leopards, 5,000 otters, 20,000 wild cats and 20,000 foxes, according to an investigative report by the Indian magazine, *Tehelka*.

During a 2006 CBI interrogation, Chand admitted selling 470 tiger skins and 2,130 leopard skins to just four clients from Nepal and Tibet. His statement revealed a saga of wildlife genocide. For preservationists, the report read like a horror story about poachers on the prowl.

Newspaper reports further stated that Surajpal had earlier worked with Chand, earning a reputation as the best supplier of tiger skins and bones. Surajpal's modus operandi was simple and deadly: poison the tigers and try to pass off their demise as stemming from natural causes.

Reports indicate that the poacher's network operated across India as a syndicate, targeting forests and reserves, almost always staying one step ahead of the law. The case of Surajpal recalls memories of India's legendary brigand from the south, Veerappan, whose legacy lives on across the country and in wildlife sanctuaries such as the Jim Corbett National Park, Rajaji National Park, Sariska Tiger Reserve, Ranthambore National Park, Pench National Park, Bandhavgarh National Park, Simlipal National Park, Melghat Tiger Reserve, and the Kaziranga National Park, among others.

Surajpal had set up a network of poachers, smugglers and brigands across India. According to the 2010 National Tiger Census, the population of Indian tigers, which was estimated at 1,706, would have been 2,500-plus, but for the illegal activities of poachers such as Surajpal. I believe that poachers like Surajpal and Chand should be tried for 'wildlife genocide' and severely punished. Chand, who was terminally ill, died in March 2014 at a hospital in Jaipur, Rajasthan, while undergoing trial.

In 2013, I organised a panel in Kolkata featuring my book, *The Safari: A Diary on Ranthambore*. The panel consisted of two prominent Indian wildlife conservationists, Belinda Wright, Executive Director of the Wildlife Protection Society of India (WPSI), and Nitin Desai, Director of WPSI Central India bureau.

We discussed the dwindling tiger population in India and talked about the much-needed conservation measures.

Mr Desai shared some counter-poaching strategies, including the Secret Information Reward Scheme, adopted by his organisation and other conservation groups. The scheme involves taking into confidence and rewarding villagers and local residents for sharing information on poachers. Establishing such networks of *mukhbirs*, or informants, from among villagers, members of various tribes and forest dwellers has already begun to pay off.

A day after our panel, Ms Wright, Mr Desai and I visited the Sundarbans. The Sundarbans National Park, Tiger and Biosphere Reserve is a UNESCO World Heritage Site. It is situated in the Sundarbans delta between India and Bangladesh, occupying 36,000 hectares. The Park is home to the Royal Bengal Tiger, one of the most elusive creatures on Earth.

Through various community services and school activities, Ms Wright and Mr Desai educated the local population about the importance of confronting poaching. Providing information about poachers is perhaps the most important aspect in tiger conservation efforts in a region that is among the most inhospitable mangrove habitats in the world. Winning the hearts of local residents appears to be the most effective weapon in tiger protection.

Although India has made great strides in its recent conservation efforts, there is no room for complacency.

Challenges remain immense, but with the energy and ability of conservationists like Mr Desai and Ms Wright, environmental activist and writer Bittu Sahgal and many others, we still have hope. I have also come to realise the efficacy of community participation in such conservation programmes.

There is growing public awareness of human rights violations around the world. It is high time that we have 'animal rights' at par with human rights under the purview of law.

UN Chronicle

September 2014

60

Click Bait

I was recently at a party in Kolkata that was attended by the who's who of the city. I go to over 300 parties and events in a year, hosted by various individuals and organisations, and meet many people — some for the first time and others who are already well-known to me — and very often people take photographs. Quite often, I run into people I don't know very well but who seem to know quite a lot about me.

I shall, however, remember this party for a very different reason, one I have rarely faced before. Let me recount what happened. As the party got going, the host came up and said he wanted me to meet somebody. Nothing unusual about that. So, I followed him.

What happened next was very unexpected. My host introduced me to someone, an industrialist who is known to me but with whom I had not been on talking terms for several years. At that moment, like any two civilised people caught in a somewhat awkward and unforeseen situation, we engaged in formal small talk, and a photographer who was nearby clicked our picture together. The whole thing was over in a few seconds.

The next day, some local newspapers carried that particular picture. The fact that I was not on talking terms with that gentleman was quite well-known in my social circles and to some others in Kolkata.

I am sure you can imagine what happened next. From early morning I started getting phone calls and text messages from friends and acquaintances, some 'congratulating' me, others whose curiosity had been piqued. Had we patched up? Was it only a photo-op? Who was the peacenik, who brokered the meet? Who took the first step? Who blinked first? Many sent the picture to others who hadn't glimpsed it yet; and a Twitter storm followed.

It is often said that a picture speaks a thousand words. But I have now realised that this isn't always true, and that a picture can often be very misleading, and in fact, can be used (misused?) to get the desired effect. All those who see a picture or photograph are usually not aware of the circumstances in which it may have been taken.

It made me wonder about the recent photographs of Salman Khan and Shah Rukh Khan meeting in similar circumstances (an Iftar party) and exchanging greetings.

Newspapers big and small carried pictures of that moment when the two mega stars hugged each other, seemingly portraying the message that there had been a patch-up between the two. After all, seeing is believing, right?

But now I know that such pictures can be very deceptive, and entirely misleading. Every now and then a photograph pops up which creates controversies. Celebrities, VIPs and even Prime Ministers are not spared. There have been so many instances when the appearance of a particular person in the same frame with a celebrity or a VIP has raised a major hullabaloo in various circles.

In the run-up to the recent Lok Sabha elections, the Congress had shared with the media photographs of BJP PM nominee Narendra Modi with an alleged hawala operator among a group of people, including other BJP leaders. The fact is that a political leader participates in hundreds of functions and events, where thousands of pictures are clicked at random. It is impossible to determine who should be in the frame when these photographs are taken. There are always perils involved in being photographed. Certain photographs may even compromise a person's dignity and tarnish their reputation. The higher the celebrity quotient, the greater the risk.

There was a recent article in London's *The Guardian* newspaper that highlighted the perils of being a stock shot model. Stock shots are photographs that illustrate general themes and are supplied to magazines, advertisers or anybody else desiring a library of useful images. The story was that a model one day found her stock shot being used in a newspaper's agony aunt column with the headline: 'I fantasize about group sex with old, obese men.' The picture of the model used by the newspaper was actually shot a few years ago for a theme which had to do with a 'cold and illness' shoot.

At the Jaipur Literature Festival's inaugural dinner earlier this year, the Rambagh Palace Hotel engaged its own photographers for the event, who later shared select photographs with the media.

With the arrival of digital devices like Google Glass, which may become commonplace like mobile phones within a few years, there are already growing world-wide privacy concerns. The wearers of Google Glass need only give a verbal command or press a button at the top of the device to start recording. People who want to take photos can do so by winking with their right eye. No need to pull out a camera or a mobile phone.

Your photo might get clicked without you even realising it, let alone giving permission or consent.

So, the next time you are at a party and an innocuous-looking person points his/her camera phone at you, take it seriously, for you never know what may happen next.

Meanwhile, The Asian Age
September 4, 2014

61

Santhara: A Ritual that Should Be Allowed to Die

Not too many people outside the Jain community knew about santhara until about a week ago. But recently, the Rajasthan High Court pronounced it illegal, and santhara became front page news.

The court order has evoked strong reactions from religious leaders and scholars from the Jain community. The order came nine years after a PIL was filed against the practice of santhara. Santhara (referred to by Shwetambars) or sallekhana (referred to by Digambars) has been described in Jain scriptures as a religious fast unto death.

"When all the purposes of life have been served or when the body becomes unable to serve any purpose, I wish to be able to adapt santhara, a religious fast unto death" — is what most of its adherents say. It was originally considered a ritual for saints who desired to desert their physical body to earn 'moksha'. It is believed that Mahavir, the 24th Tirthankara of Jainism, had left his body through santhara.

According to certain scholars, the greatest ascetic discipline in the tradition is the rite of santhara or sallekhana — voluntary self-starvation in a systematic manner over a 12-year period. It combines the mandate of both asceticism and non-injury, since the eating of food, even of plants, and the drinking of water entail the ingestion and killing of vegetables and micro-organic life.

The fully-committed Jain monk is obliged to sweep the path before him lest he step on an insect; to strain his water and to avoid movement in the dark, and even to refrain from bathing, since such actions might harm insects and organic life. When final and complete purification is attained, the soul rises to a transcendental realm of pure omniscience far above the highest heavens — even above the gods. Or so goes the traditional belief.

What it might be in reality is a little different. This ritual attracted some international attention in 2006, when a 93-year-old Bimla Devi Hirawat, embraced santhara. Human rights activist and lawyer Nikhil Soni and another counsel filed a PIL in the Rajasthan High Court, and one of the main arguments put forward was that it is usually old people who resort to santhara, and that it is inhumane to let a person die without medical assistance, food or water.

Soni grew up in Churu, Rajasthan, the same place where I was born and spent my childhood, and the same district that has now acquired the dubious reputation of being the santhara capital of the world — known for the highest per capita incidence of this practice in recent years. In fact, my extended family also has a history of santhara.

In 2006, Soni heard of Bimla Devi, who was diagnosed with terminal cancer and who was coerced into santhara by her family. In her final hours, as she started screaming for water, her cries were drowned out by loud bhajans accompanied with *dholaks*. That year, after failing to get the police to prevent Bimla Devi's demise through santhara, Soni filed a writ petition in the Rajasthan High Court against the practice. Calling it a 'social evil' that should be deemed an act of suicide, and therefore, illegal under Indian law, his petition demands that practitioners of santhara should be prosecuted under Section 309 of the Indian Penal Code for 'attempt to commit suicide' and that their supporters, and those who encourage it by venerating them as 'spiritually elevated' beings, should be, charged with abetting a crime.

I would not, however, accept as some critics do, that santhara can be compared with ritualised murder — an act devised to rid the family of the economic burden of taking care of its aged and unproductive members. I had said as much in an interview with *Radio Washington* recently.

This age-old ritual can be compared to another ritual that has been glorified over the ages — namely, sati. Again, the practice was found to be quite common in Rajasthan. In 1987, when 18-year-old Roop Kanwar died on her husband's pyre, there was an outcry and finally the administration buckled under pressure and prevented people from going to the site and glorifying the heinous act.

A short film on the issue of santhara recently won numerous awards. Its director, Shekhar Hattangadi, has brought the focus sharply on this intersection of religion, law and constitutional secularism. The Mumbai-based journalist/filmmaker says, "Santhara for me is a classic example of the challenge that all faith-based societies face as they adopt modern, secular norms of governance. The challenge is to reconcile individual freedom and personal liberty as well as a minority community's religious rights on one hand, and the need for state intervention in matters of religion on the other. The Rajasthan High Court ruling has angered a sizeable chunk of the Jain community as they neither deem it suicide nor do they call it euthanasia."

To believers in santhara, it is the highest form of

meditation, and they feel that their position has not been properly represented in court; hence they plan to move the Supreme Court against the ban in the near future.

The Asian Age & The Times of India

August 18, 2015

62

R.I.P. Tigress Queen of Ranthambore

It was not that I was not getting news of Machhli — she had not been eating over the last four-five days. I get a stream of updates from Ranthambore daily because of my personal passion and interest in wildlife. But as soon as I got the expected news of Machhli's demise, I felt a terrible loss — almost personal.

My relationship with this tigress dates back several years. That's why this tragic news forced me to make a couple of phone calls to reconfirm. Why not? She has cheated death so many times in the past. Every time I went to Ranthambore, my aim was to see Machhli and compare her with pictures from when I saw her last. The beautiful tigress was named so because of the marks on her face that resembled fish. She was indeed the most sought-after, and hence the most photographed big cat.

Machhli's life story is nothing short of amazing. She

has come out of the jaws of death several times — the most talked about is her fierce battle with a crocodile that later led to the loss of her two canines, but she otherwise remained unscathed. Despite all her battles, she managed to defy the usual lifespan of a tiger, which is not more than 15 years. Machhli was almost 20!

Machhli, with her large family consisting of 11 cubs, of which seven were females, is related by blood to most tigers found in the forests of Rajasthan. As a result, the tigress won several sobriquets such as 'Queen Mother of the Tigers', 'Lady of the Lakes' or 'Tigress Queen of Ranthambore'. It is said that she alone brought in revenue worth more than $10 million every year, such was the fame and magnetic pull of her majestic looks.

She ruled over a large kingdom and it is said that even tigers were intimidated by her because of her strength. Several films were shot, and several books were written about her. A darling of animal lovers, she has also managed to bag an award for herself — the TOFT Lifetime Achievement Award for her contribution to conservation.

I have heard people regretting not seeing her on their visits to Ranthambore and how this failure to spot her would make them go back. There have been many times when she could not be sighted for days at a stretch. During this period of absence, people would often apprehend that, perhaps, she had died somewhere. With her age factor, failing health, even fights with her own cubs, she perhaps preferred to lie low. But then again, when she was sighted once more, animal lovers rejoiced.

Of late, forest officials fed her as she was unable to hunt much and would remain hungry. With the death of Machhli or T-16, a curtain falls, marking the end of an era.

Not only Ranthambore, but the entire wildlife of the country has lost a sparkling jewel. With her no more, will Ranthambore have the same charm for Machhli fans and animal lovers all over the world? R.I.P Machhli. We will miss you.

Meanwhile, The Asian Age

August 30, 2016

63

MEA to Exempt Infants from Passport Seva Kendras

It was such a big relief to learn that the Ministry of External Affairs has finally issued an Office Memorandum dated September 28, 2017, exempting children below five years and physically disabled persons with amputated hands from biometric registration during obtaining a passport.

I had sensed the seriousness of the matter when I applied for a passport for my infant daughter, only a few months old at the time, and was told by my travel agent that she had to appear in person at the passport office. I came to know that much to the consternation of parents, an infant born in India, as per the extant norms, has to be taken to the Passport Seva Kendra (PSK) office in order to comply with the formalities of getting a passport. I talked to the regional passport officer and was told that I had no other option but to comply with it — which meant taking my daughter to the PSK.

The very idea of taking my baby to a PSK was immensely worrying. Parents, like myself, who find themselves in such a situation are naturally anxious. Since the PSK offices are visited by innumerable people, maintaining a proper sanitised environment that is conducive for infants, and where they are not exposed to diseases and infections, is usually not possible.

Quite surprised with this norm in India, I spoke to a few diplomat friends and came to know that the physical presence of infants is not required in getting passports in many countries. I also came to know that most of the foreign missions in India do not require the infant's presence or their fingerprints for issuing visas.

There are millions of Indians working outside India who come back to the country for maternity leave or some other reason and have to return to work at the earliest. These people would inevitably face the hassle of taking their babies to passport offices as it was necessary for them to get a passport for their newborns.

Extremely perturbed by this highly inconvenient regulation, I decided to write to the Minister of External Affairs (MEA) Smt Sushma Swaraj. In my letter dated June 27, 2017, I had requested the minister to take up this matter and work out a mechanism to issue passports for newborns in such a manner so that they are not exposed to any risk. I also wrote in my letter that there is a need to re-evaluate the necessity of fingerprinting newborns and work out viable alternatives.

Thereafter, I went and met Smt Sushma Swaraj in person. I also met many other senior officials to press home the point that there was an urgent need to change the rules since taking young children to PSKs raised potentially critical issues around health and hygiene. Moreover, doctors say that the fingerprints of newborns take at least two to three years to fully take shape. So, the entire exercise, as it existed, was quite redundant.

The MEA order in response to my letter has been welcomed by many and I thank our Foreign Minister, Smt Sushma Swaraj, for taking prompt action on my letter, as she has been doing on many other issues during her tenure.

I must thank Minister of State Mr Hardeep Singh Puri for his personal intervention and full support extended to me on the matter.

I am glad that going forward thousands of parents in India, out to procure a passport for their babies, can heave a collective sigh of relief.

sundeepbhutoria.blogspot.com

October 1, 2017

64

An Open Letter to the Prime Minister of India

Even as West Bengal is gearing up for a stricter lockdown from 5pm today, many people are trying to find a job to survive. This includes many artists and craftspeople who are not financially stable.

I have been, and am still, receiving a number of phone calls and feelers regarding the thousands of folk artists, craftspeople and artisans who are facing immense hardships in light of the pandemic to eke out a living. These are all individuals who earn their livelihood by promoting Indian culture and heritage. Even during normal times, these unsung torchbearers of Indianness struggle to make ends meet. What is happening now has thrust them from the frying pan into the fire.

In the wake of the Covid-19 pandemic, artisans and artists who live hand-to-mouth have been desperate to support their families and somehow keep themselves and their traditional crafts and skills alive.

People like me are very concerned about this situation as several traditional folk arts of India had already started fading away pre-pandemic, with the poor artisans unable to keep up with the times. This, I was told, threatened to wipe out vast swathes of India's cultural capital and heritage accumulated over thousands of years.

As our organisation, Prabha Khaitan Foundation, with its associates, regularly works with folk artists across India, I was very worried about their well-being. The scale of the pandemic's impact has been so big that only a concerted government effort could ameliorate their situation. So, finding no proper solution, I decided to write an open letter to the Prime Minister of India, with a copy to the Culture Minister, highlighting the plight of the artisans and craftspeople and requesting for a scheme to bring them all under one protective umbrella.

The Prime Minister's Office was very prompt in acknowledging my letter and also acted upon it by forwarding it to the department concerned.

A few days later, I got a letter a letter from Shri Prahlad Singh Patel, Minister of State for Culture and Tourism, Government of India, who assured me that his ministry had written to all the Zonal Cultural Centres of India to empanel the names of all artisans — even those who had not been empanelled earlier — for government support.

I was not sure what exactly the support to these artisans and craftspeople would constitute. Therefore, I also wrote to all the directors of the Zonal Cultural Centres. I am confident that the authorities will eventually take positive steps to help the most vulnerable in these trying times.

I must thank Mr Maneesh Tripathi and Ms Shazia Ilmi for extending their support and standing by me in articulating the cause of folk artists and craftspeople.

sundeepbhutoria.blogspot.com

July 9, 2020

65

Kindergarteners and the Perils of Online Education

It was a moment of great relief when I saw the tweet of Human Resources Development (HRD) Minister Ramesh Pokhriyal, also known as 'Nishank', on July 14, 2020, stating that the Government of India had passed a set of guidelines called *Pragyata* mandating that the maximum screen time for online education should be three hours per day. Further, the guidelines dictate that kids in pre-primary classes should not spend more than 30 minutes on online learning.

This HRD Ministry guideline has, to a great extent, addressed the concerns of thousands of parents across India whose children are kindergarteners. Compelled by the need for social distancing norms in the wake of the Covid-19 pandemic, the whole world is trying to evolve to a new online educational paradigm. Though an essential step that cannot be avoided, I am strongly against any system that compels tiny tots to spend extended screen time on computers and laptops for education.

The world has to adapt and change with the times, and as such, the pedagogical changes taking place with online education mostly constitute moving up the social evolutionary ladder, but the perils of such a system must also be taken into account. All endeavours must be put in place to ensure that no harm is done to those who are taking their first steps as learners. If, as a result of relentless online classes, the foundation of education among toddlers becomes weak, the long-term learning outcomes can never be positive.

I, being the father of a young daughter, feel very deeply about this subject and decided to take up this issue with the Government of India by writing letters to the departments concerned.

Notwithstanding the revolutionary promise of schooling from one's living room, I am sure thousands of parents, like myself, are concerned about the adverse impact of online education on the tender minds of their children.

sundeepbhutoria.blogspot.com

July 19, 2020

66

Why are 'Fat Cats' Being So Reckless in Covid Times?

- A group of 30 revellers at a destination wedding return to Kolkata and test Covid-positive. Some have to be hospitalised.
- A gang of friends goes to a nearby resort to celebrate an anniversary and 10 out of 12 test positive; one of them succumbs to the deadly virus. And yet...

Every star hotel banquet in town is booked for a wedding, an anniversary, a birthday... name it and you have it. One star hotel is brimming over with about hundred honeymooning couples and every hand on the kitchen deck is busy whipping up anniversary cakes.

I just cannot reconcile with what is going on.

What is happening to us?

Even as the coronavirus sends the world reeling, more and more invitations for weddings and social events pile up on my desk. This is causing acute FOBI (fear of being included) in me. Every invitation seems to be an open challenge to put my own and my family's life at risk. For the vast majority in my social circle, FOMO (fear of missing out) continues to be the mantra behind compulsive mingling.

Make no mistake, I am not alone in the FOBI group. There are others I know who feel anxious at being invited to group or social events now. A recent invitation from a friend asking me to his wife's 35th birthday celebration left me dumbfounded, more so because my polite refusal was rejected! Acquaintances, schooled in traditional rules of etiquette, refuse to take 'no' for an answer and insist you must be there. This *ati aachar* or extreme behaviour is nothing short of emotional *atyachaar* (torture).

One can understand when poor, illiterate citizens cannot comply with Covid-19 norms out of necessity. Work from home is a luxury that not many can afford, and nine months into the pandemic, financial compulsions have forced a vast majority out into the world to keep food on the table.

But when educated social 'fat cats' use their clout to flout the pandemic rules for their own merriment, it causes far more harm to society. All those messages and campaigns urging people to maintain social distancing seem to go down the drain. It also provokes resentment in several quarters as it puts society's inequalities in full public view.

As a result, hotels and travel agencies are facing a grim dichotomy: while having to cope with declining revenues and job cuts, they also have to contend with clients who have scant respect for regulations and often use their influence to bend the rules.

I know about mega weddings in star hotels where a limited number of visitors are allowed as per pandemic rules. One organiser, not to be curbed by these restrictions, booked three banquets in different names on the same day at the same hotel. On the day of the wedding, stunned hotel authorities watched guests from three different venues converge at the spot where the ceremony was taking place, in blatant violation of social distancing norms. Such an ingenious yet irresponsible formula has become quite common now, unquestioningly accepted by most.

I know of so many people who have been organising easily-avoidable public gatherings and events with a business-as-usual approach. It is, as if, there has been a lockdown on one's reasoning. We've all seen pictures on social media of crowded Goa nightclubs with no hint of Covid-19 precautions. I was even more stunned to see on television a crowd marching hand-in-hand, many of them without masks, to spread awareness about... coronavirus!

The Delhi government has increased fines for not wearing facemasks in public to ₹2,000, to help check the spread of the disease. But for the rich and (often) infamous, this is hardly a deterrent.

The rush to circumvent rules is like an epidemic in itself. Political rallies, holidaying, weddings and social gatherings during a crisis like this reveal an attitude that reeks of arrogance and downright stupidity.

One of the primary advantages of being educated is the ability it gives us to connect and reason the cause and effect of events. But in a society where money, influence and hubris rank higher than reasoning, our very survival is at stake.

The world over, this pandemic debate has been about the two Ls: Life and Livelihood. I would like to add a third L: Lunacy.

What else can explain our crazy compulsion for hosting and attending social functions when a pandemic is at its peak?

The Asian Age

December 24, 2020

67

Remedy against Cultural Colonisation

Diwali 2020 was an unusual one, like the whole year, bereft of all the revelry that accompany the festival of lights. I took the opportunity of a quiet holiday to tell my little daughter Aavya the story of Lord Ram and why we celebrate Diwali. Imagine my consternation then, when a few weeks later she marched up to me and demanded, "Papa, where is my Christmas tree?"

I was stumped. How did my three-year-old child know about this holiday? And, why in heaven's name was she *this* excited about a Christmas tree? Then the peppa, er penny dropped — like almost every preschooler of her generation, Aavya was hooked to the British animated series, *Peppa Pig*.

I have always felt very strongly about new generations learning the stories of their own land before learning about other cultures. The influence exerted on young minds by shows like *Peppa Pig* is a huge cause for concern. When

I shared my thoughts with my friend Anant Vijay, the National Award-winning writer of Hindi literature, film critic and columnist, he echoed my views. He subsequently penned a very pertinent piece on cultural colonialism in Hindi in his weekly column in *Dainik Jagran*. I would like to, with his kind permission, reproduce an English translation of this article by Anant Vijay.

∾

CHRISTMAS just got over and I was catching up with one of my friends during that period. He told me, just three days before Christmas his three-year-old daughter asked him, "Where is my Christmas tree?" Prior to that, he had often related to me incidents about how his daughter bartered and bartered to watch a cartoon show in lieu of doing her daily chores like brushing her teeth. He seemed worried about the immense impact of cartoons on children but now that his daughter demanded a "Christmas tree", he was quite disturbed and wondered whether in the future, a day might come when children would say, "Today is Sunday, let's go to church."

After lending an ear to his concern, I realised there is definitely a pertinent issue to ponder here. Meanwhile, I interacted with another friend, who had a similar tale. He was concerned about his two-year-old kid picking up a very funny and foreign pronunciation and insisting on saying "shews" instead of "shoes". It was evident from both conversations with my friends that their children were hooked to the popular British animated series, *Peppa Pig*, on YouTube.

The pandemic-induced year-long lockdown has compelled children to stay away from schools and outdoor activities and they have been forced to spend more time in the digital world. Animated television series like *Peppa Pig* have gained immense popularity globally during this period. There is an exclusive YouTube channel that telecasts the show and millions of children watch the episodes intently.

Peppa Pig is four years old and has a brother, George. They live with their parents, Mummy Pig and Daddy Pig. Children are obsessed with the show. *Peppa Pig* has attained iconic status and is marketed in children's items as motif on school bags, lunch boxes, water bottles, pencil boxes et al. As I spoke to a large number of parents of pre-school-going children, they often confessed that they were indebted to Peppa Pig, who came in handy when their children refused to eat or threw tantrums. They would immediately revert to an episode of the show that depicts something related to sudden and illogical outbursts and the children would comply to obey their parents. A UK-based company creates the show and regularly uploads the latest episodes of *Peppa Pig* on YouTube.

At the outset, there is nothing unnatural about the craze for the series. There is a strong debate in favour of this preschool series that argues about the positive effect it has on children by inculcating family values and bonding. It also brings to the fore the fact that at a time when the very concept of "family" was disintegrating in Britain, the *Peppa Pig* series was strategically placed to highlight the qualities of a happy, healthy family.

The series became an instant hit but one must remember that these videos were created keeping in mind the social, religious and cultural background of the land and to specifically cater to children in the UK. But if we analyse the observation of my friends in the instances mentioned earlier, one thing emerges clearly — these shows may have a long-term detrimental effect on the children's psyche.

Children in India are being impacted by shows that are not Indian in any way and are, in fact, distancing our children from our indigenous culture. It is time to consider this pertinent issue and evaluate if such shows are actually harmful for our little children and will these shows accelerate an erosion of our cultural ethos.

At this point, the media is being utilised as a weapon to promote the positive aspects of a welfare state and hence, it is necessary to keep a strict vigil on the quality of the contents. With state-of-the-art technological know-how as its handmaid, this is the latest trend adopted by colonialists to enforce their cultural and religious supremacy and plant the roots of colonisation on the unsuspecting victim.

The things that children in our country are learning from *Peppa Pig* point in this direction. Child psychology also reiterates that children are immensely influenced by the virtual world and tend to see the actual world as an extension of that make-believe world. This may not affect their intellect but it definitely influences their social behaviour, and when social behaviour is affected, it percolates down to tradition, affecting cultural behaviour as well.

Recently, the Government of India sent very detailed and specific instructions to different ministries about its curated and non-curated content regulation policy. All curated content beamed on video streaming platforms or over the top (OTT) platforms were brought under the purview of the Information and Broadcasting Ministry. Non-curated content platforms, including Facebook and YouTube, were brought under the Ministry of Electronics and Information Technology. This was done for better vigilance on the quality of the contents and also to keep a check whether the platforms were adhering to guidelines in the contents they beam.

If any content shown on YouTube is found to influence or impact Indian culture in any way, the government should take up the issue with utmost firmness. This is vital because we have already witnessed the consequence when the Congress party outsourced the nation's cultural and ancillary wings to the Leftists. During that phase, Kalidas' plays were undermined by Anton Chekov's plays and Maxim Gorky's *Mother* was given precedence over Premchand's *Godan*. It resulted in our swift cultural downfall. As a result, we failed to reach the heights of growth and excellence in the spheres of national education, language, literature and culture.

Owing to the thrust given to the spread of English, it became easier for the West to establish its colonial hold on modern India. This affected children as well. The rich treasure trove of children's literature in different regional Indian languages was shoved under the carpet and replaced by English literary works. It is now necessary to counter the way technology is being used to subvert Indian culture.

For this, it is necessary to create world-class indigenous content for children and beam them widely across various platforms, including YouTube. This entire process needs concrete planning and has to be accelerated. Interesting stories and characters highlighting Indian traditions and values have to be picked up and presented in an engaging manner to attract children. There are many characters in the stories of the Puranas that are positive and inspiring and have the potential to be close to children's hearts.

It is now the need of the hour to pick up those characters, enhance their positive aspects and bring them to the fore for contemporary children with the aid of the latest technological know-how. This will require a proper set-up and expertise to produce quality shows. It is not easy for an individual to attain the quality of content and production that *Peppa Pig* has reached, it requires huge financial and human resources. Individual efforts are seen here and there but these are inadequate and have not been able to impact the entertainment market in any way.

It has been more than seven decades since Independence, but we have failed to do any concrete work around Indian culture. To Commemorate the 75th anniversary of Independence, a number of Bollywood bigwigs announced their decision to make films that highlight Indian tradition and culture. Producer-director Karan Johar announced his resolution on Twitter and tagged Prime Minister Narendra Modi. It is necessary for established producers like Johar to consider creating interesting content for Indian children. Original Indian characters should be created who propagate Indian tradition and culture. If we can do this successfully, not only can we save ourselves from falling prey to cultural imperialism but it will also help our future generations to get connected to and remain proud of our very own heritage.

sundeepbhutoria.blogspot.com

Anant Vijay's column was originally published in Hindi in *Dainik Jagran* on December 27, 2020

Literature

Dedicated to

***Jaipur** — the Pink City*

ना यह शहर मुझे थकाता है...
ना मैं इस शहर से थकता हूँ

"That's the thing about books. They let you travel without moving your feet."

– Jhumpa Lahiri

68

When JLF Comes, Can Controversies be Far Behind?

Jaipur Literature Festival (JLF) is the mother of all literary festivals in India. The very concept of JLF has directly and indirectly inspired over a hundred such festivals of different hues across India and beyond. However, none can match it in terms of stature or reach.

I find myself agreeing with the organisers when they say Jaipur Lit Fest is the biggest free literary festival in the world. Another unique feature of JLF has been the lit fest getting embroiled in one controversy or the other. In fact, people often say, "if JLF comes, can controversies be far behind?"

Whether it is an invite sent to Salman Rushdie in 2012 or Ashis Nandy's statement on Dalits and corruption that created a furore, or for that matter, a native-versus-foreigner spat between author William Dalrymple and former editor of *Open* magazine, Hartosh Singh Bal.

Some poets thought it fit to read out excerpts from Rushdie's *Satanic Verses* and had to flee from Jaipur overnight when FIRs were lodged. That's not just it. There is more. A bottle was hurled at Ekta Kapoor in the Front Lawn by a member of an activist organisation.

Last year's JLF, however, was relatively quiet, with no rain to play spoilsport or no banned books to read from or no Vikram Seth to sip his red wine on the stage while in conversation.

As I landed in Jaipur yesterday, I wondered what lay in store this time at JLF. I had a gut feeling that this year's JLF would be quieter, with sun-kissed mornings discussing art, literature, history, theatre and so on.

In the evening, at the *Jaipur Times* Food & Nightlife Awards, I heard that a public interest litigation (PIL) had been filed against the organisers for not finding a suitable venue in terms of security and traffic. The hearing is on Wednesday. The organisers are working overtime to frame their line of argument in court as to why Diggi Palace is a hassle-free venue with respect to the traffic and security.

So, is JLF going to be in the news once again, not only for its literary and organisational merit, but also its line-up of authors and selection of programmes?

Coming back to the *Jaipur Times* Food & Nightlife Awards 2016 function, I met quite a lot of known

Jaipurites. Though many say that with more and more booklovers and fest visitors thronging the sessions, Diggi Palace as a venue seems smaller. The fact, however, is that the venue has increased in space with more room for seating, standing, or simply strolling.

Moreover, in order to reduce the pressure on the centrally located Diggi Palace, the cultural events have been shifted to Hotel Clarks Amer, and the tourism and cultural events to Amber Fort and Albert Hall.

For me, though, JLF would remain incomplete without the heritage and charm of Diggi Palace.

sundeepbhutoria.blogspot.com

January 19, 2016

69

Book Viewing Versus Book Buying

I could not spend much time at Jaipur Lit Fest yesterday as I had to host an Ek Mulakat event with the Jayshree Periwal Foundation at the ITC Rajputana in the afternoon. Javed Akhtar was in conversation with Sangeeta Datta on her album *Anant*. Sangeeta sang well and Javed Akhtar was, as usual, popular among the Jaipurites.

I hardly slept a wink last night because it was 2.30am by the time I finished dinner, hosted by Prabha Khaitan Foundation in collaboration with Vani Prakashan for the Hindi and Urdu authors. By the time I got back to my room, the clock had struck 4.

So, I decided to pen my blog right away, as I would have to leave for the Vintage Car Rally flag-off ceremony at 10am the next day.

This evening's dinner was attended by all the prominent Hindi and Urdu authors of Rajasthan who had come for the lit fest. Almost all the authors, directly or indirectly, expressed their feelings against the discriminatory treatment meted out to regional authors vis-à-vis English authors. Padmashree Deval spoke about this as well. Honestly, I too have always felt this. The reason I requested Vani Prakashan to come on board with us as a host during the lit fest was to create a feel-good factor among regional authors, who might have otherwise felt left out.

It is widely known that English publication houses frequently host lavish dinners at the city's five star hotels, exclusively for English authors. No such events are ever organised for their regional counterparts.

Jaipur Literature Festival is the biggest of fests in terms of scale, quality of programmes, and the eclectic mix of writers from all over the world. The organisers take huge pride in the fact that from a small festival it has become a mammoth five-day literary jamboree with lakhs of people coming to attend.

One question, however, endures — while lakhs of people come to JLF, how many really buy books?

My experience with Jaipurites is that they love book viewing. The thronging crowds at JLF flaunt fashion, indulge in shopping for knick-knacks, drink wine and beer, and even fill up the sessions. But they rarely buy books. Some of the book stalls set up by leading publishers are waiting for the customers who swarm around the food and beverage kiosks.

Similarly, the booths selling trinkets, clothes and even pickles and chutneys, for that matter, witness much better footfall than the bookstalls. One observation that I would like to make is that the majority of the books bought at JLF are by the visitors who come to Jaipur from other places.

One of the many excuses is that the tech-savvy youth of today prefer reading on their mobile phones, laptops, and Kindles. Gone are the days when people would wear an old coat and read a new book. Nowadays people buy a designer dress or a bag rather than a book. The sad faces of the booksellers, who shell out quite a bit to set up stalls in the lit fest, reflect this hard fact. What is more astonishing is that even outlets selling fancy things like mugs and diaries attract more people than book stalls.

I had organised a book launch session of a well-known author in a luxury hotel. The elite of Jaipur was present but only about 10 copies of the book were sold, despite a discount. A sad commentary on the so-called book lovers of Jaipur.

The JLF organisers also need to ensure that the

moderators and presenters who go up on stage know the correct names of the authors and the guests while calling them to the dais.

sundeepbhutoria.blogspot.com

January 24, 2016

70

Power Dinners — Let's Play Spot the Authors

The 10th edition of Jaipur Literature Festival (JLF) takes off on Thursday, January 19, at the Diggi Palace hotel. I have been attending JLF since its inception and have closely watched it grow into an international event. Far from the madding crowd, there are these dinners that have become a very popular part of the lit fest itinerary. Some, like the Rambagh Palace dinner on the festival eve, hosted in honour of authors and celebrities, have acquired a status symbol for perfumed elites of Jaipur.

For the past three years, I have noticed the presence of the who's who of Jaipur increasing at the Rambagh Palace dinner, which earlier used to be only for authors and like-minded people. Now, it is no longer an authors-only affair, though the hotel does a fabulous job of hosting this dinner with an increasing footfall every year.

Likewise, JLF ends with the Writers' Ball, which again used to be a gala affair. I remember, when it used to be held at Amber Fort, the invitees had to flash their invitation cards much before they actually made it through the entrance. Just two years ago, nobody would check your card even at the entrance. At the Le Meridien dinner last year, one had to go around with an eyeglass to locate any authors.

Between the lit fest's opening dinner at the Taj Rambagh Palace and the concluding Writers' Ball, there are many other lavish spreads that tantalise the culinary senses. Some are formally announced, while others are closed-door exclusive events. Last year, yours truly hosted dinners for authors every evening during the lit fest at the ITC Rajputana. This year, there will be an exclusive sit-down dinner on Friday, January 20, hosted by an international publishing house at Rambagh. The same day, HarperCollins is hosting a dinner at the Amber Fort. On Saturday, January 21, for the first time, Penguin will host a dinner at the Rajmahal Hotel. The same day, Roli Books is hosting a dinner at a posh restaurant in Amber Fort, where it will also showcase Meera Ali's latest book. Apart from these 'power dinners', there are some niche private dinners being organised in and around Jaipur during the five days of the festival.

One such private dinner is being hosted by Mita and Rahul Kapur on the evening of January 19 where one can find all the famous authors. One more dinner is scheduled for the evening of January 22 at Rajkumar Tongya's residence in honour of the renowned industrialist from Nepal, Binod Chaudhary. It would be a closed-door affair.

Chief Minister Vasundhara Raje Scindia also hosts official evening dinners for a select group of authors and friends. I have also attended the tea party at the Raj Bhawan hosted by the then Governor, Margaret Alva, for the authors.

All these dinners cater to the well-known authors and celebrities. At JLF's official dinner at Hotel Clarks Amer, one hardly gets to see a known author. It is mostly the regional authors and festival delegates who attend. Last year, Padma Shri C.P. Deval lamented this fact, outraged over a dinner party on the terrace of ITC Rajputana.

There is another private dinner on the evening of January 20, to be held after the inauguration of a sculpture at the Jawahar Kala Kendra by Chief Minister Vasundhara Raje Scindia. This evening I shall, for the first time, miss out on the Taj Rambagh dinner party as I am hosting the participating authors of Kolkata Literature Festival at Taj Bengal.

Having been a regular at most of these dinners in past

years, I am trying to figure out if we can label them as 'literature for dinner' or 'dinner for literature', or neither.

Lit Nama, DNA, Jaipur

January 18, 2017

71

A Wish List for JLF

Being a regular at Jaipur Literature Festival (JLF) over the years, those of us familiar with its ways have a wish list. We pray our wishes come true in its 10th year. To begin with, it seems that one of these has already been answered. This year, there will be a cashless option with adequate facilities for easing online transactions. Let's hope the rest of our list also comes true!

The price of the famed Diggi Puri Chai in traditional *kulhad* (earthen cup) has gone up year-on-year. I wish this year the price of the chai — the most popular item at JLF — remains the same as last year. Even my modest knowledge of economics tells me that given the economy of scale, each *kulhad* will still rake in a neat profit.

I wish JLF would come up with a mechanism to stop those early-bird book lovers who come to the venue and block seats for their latecomer friends by placing bags and newspapers on seats, preventing others who come on time from getting a seat.

If you are a Jaipurite, you'd wish you don't get any calls from friends and relatives for booking hotels and procuring entry passes. You can consider yourself lucky if you have not received any such calls. With the shortage of hotel rooms and soaring rates, requests for home-stays and 'can I be your guest' are rampant during JLF season.

Another wish is that you manage to get the author to sign your copy of his book. Sometimes, the queue of signature-seekers is so long that the author is whisked off to another session before your turn arrives.

Yet another important, and personal, wish is that the organisers arrange for proper personnel to conduct sessions, especially for those featuring Hindi and regional authors. During one of the sessions in the last edition, an announcer — clearly not very familiar with Hindi terms and names — had announced the names of the book, author and publisher inappropriately. I wish this would not happen again, as it is disrespectful to our mother tongue.

Here's another wishful scenario: You are hungry but you aren't entitled to lunch since you have a normal entry pass to JLF. You might want to go back home or to your hotel, have lunch, and come back. But this is not possible, given the sea of humanity and the traffic outside. You wish that suddenly Ram Pratap Diggi appears and, in his inimitable style, asks you for lunch by making the lunch area accessible!

In the times of Swachh Bharat, we wish the washrooms are at least usable, if not immaculately clean. Also, you wake up early, get ready, reach the venue on time all the while wishing that the gates for the session would still be open.

Last but not the least, on a serious note, I wish that the organisers provide adequate facilities for the elderly and visitors with special needs so that they too can experience a hassle-free JLF.

Lit Nama, DNA, Jaipur

January 19, 2017

72

Front Lawn — the Heart of JLF

Jaipur Literature Festival has a certain cachet that other literature festivals lack. Along with the authors and litterateurs, it has attracted the who's who of Jaipur as well as from other cities. From reading sessions to book-signings, debates to dinners, the lit fest has spawned a popular subculture of its own, attracting thousands of enthusiasts.

Though all the venues are mostly packed, the Front Lawn of the historic Diggi Palace is the largest and most popular at the lit fest. The Front Lawn's unique appeal stems from the fact that the most famous authors have their events here. Right from the inaugural session to the finale, all major events take place at the Front Lawn. One such event is the much-awaited debate with which the lit fest concludes.

The debate itself can become controversial. Last year, it stirred up a controversy when a renowned cine star, in a verbal sally, shocked the audience by using choicest of invectives in Hindi.

Visitors, geared with water bottles and snacks, come and occupy the seats much in advance for the first literary session of each day. Then there are those who plant themselves at the Front Lawn and sit through the entire day's sessions that take place.

The Front Lawn is a symbolic representation of the entire venue of the heritage property and the mood of the lit fest — large crowds, book lovers, dating couples and so on. While some are engrossed in the discussions in right earnest, others, especially the backbenchers, take a nap in the warm winter sun. Young couples are often seen in their own sessions of romantic tete-a-tete in blissful oblivion.

During the initial years of the lit fest, there used to be around 150 to 200 enthusiasts at the Front Lawn. Now it has increased ten-fold. The Front Lawn has been host to some of the biggest names like Amitabh Bachchan, Dev Anand, Naseeruddin Shah, Oprah Winfrey, Gulzar, Javed Akhtar, Sonam Kapoor and the august presence of writers like Orhan Pamuk, V.S. Naipaul, Kiran Desai, Michael

Cunningham and Margaret Atwood, among others.

The five-day lit fest at the Front Lawn invariably begins with a musical session in the morning and is followed by one-on-one talks and group discussions throughout the day. There is a book launch in the evening.

The Lawn has the famous Diggi Puri ki Chai, where most people catch up with one another. The entrance to the media terrace, authors' lounge, lunch area and even Room 506, which I used to have for the past few years, is accessible from here. This year, too, I had booked this room well in advance. From the verandah of this room, one can listen to the Front Lawn sessions. I use this room for my media interviews and meetings with the authors. Many of my friends and authors freshen up here as well.

However, despite booking in advance and having paid a premium over last year's rates, the Diggi Palace officials informed my team that they cannot give me the room. The reason is best known to them. My team was told that the room was not to be allotted but blocked for some VIP movement. I was surprised to hear that, as JLF had started this most appreciable culture among such events in the country of first-come-first-served and had even denied entry to the then HRD minister, Kapil Sibal, after the gates were closed.

Thanks to the intervention of Sanjoy Roy, we have

Room 111 now, which luckily is also accessible from the Front Lawn.

sundeepbhutoria.blogspot.com

* An excerpt from this blog post appeared in *Lit Nama, DNA,* Jaipur, on January 20, 2017

73

It's a Fashion Jamboree

The stupendous growth of Jaipur Literature Festival (JLF) has extended its boundaries beyond authors, books and reading sessions. Not only is it in vogue to be present, but also being in style is important. In fact, many aptly call it a 'fashion jamboree', where trends in apparel and accessories draw as many eyeballs as the fest's literary activities.

With the young brigade clad in colourful and chic scarves, overcoats, boots and leather jackets, beautifully complemented by chunky accessories like psychedelic glasses, bowler hats, dangling earrings, choker neckwear and a variety of bracelets, one gets an eyeful.

It's the right venue and weather for women to use their pashminas and, of course, for a selective few, tooshes and jamewars. Men are spotted mostly in Nehru or Modi-style jackets. Sunglasses are a must for all. The only thing I am yet to spot is a world-renowned brand of diaries or notebooks. While I spot hundreds of Louis Vuitton, Gucci,

Prada, Salvatore Ferragamo and Burberry handbags, I'm yet to spot a single leather Smith or Sotheby's notebook or even a *Financial Times* diary.

Also, I guess a formal three-piece suit and tie are an absolute no-no at JLF. I was surprised when my friends from Kolkata, and even a few from London, who were visiting JLF for the first time, wanted to know what clothes they should pack. They didn't once mention the weather and were more interested in making a style statement. The regular visiting authors also have their distinctive styles. Shashi Tharoor dons smart Nehru jackets with matching pocket squares and his shirts have eye-catching cuff-links. Gulzar and Javed Akhtar wear their trademark long kurtas and pyjamas. Javed is usually seen in a jacket, with a shawl flowing down from his shoulders.

William Dalrymple loves wearing trousers with short kurtas. Sanjoy is seen with ethnic printed shirts and sleeveless jackets. Navtej Sarna loves wearing overcoats, given the January Jaipur winter. The ever-graceful Jyotika Diggi is always in her traditional attire, which speaks for the family's culture and tradition. Top marks to authors who have their native handloom bags and hat or muffler that reflect the heritage of the region they belong to.

JLF currently is about high fashion and a sartorial display, including funky trinkets, ethnic apparel, upbeat eyewear, colourful headgear and so on.

My designer friend Rohit Kamra receives several inquiries from Jaipurites on the fashion trends doing the rounds of JLF and what to wear. It could be for the event or for the dinners or the grand finale, something that would differentiate one from the crowd, yet provide an intellectual look.

Lit Nama, DNA, Jaipur

January 21, 2017

74

What Makes a Festival Click

We must give credit to JLF for spreading the culture of literature festivals across India. Many cities, big and small, seem to have taken a leaf out of the success of JLF and started their own.

Even the book fairs in Delhi and Kolkata have started literature festivals on the sidelines of the main fair. Many people have asked who is actually responsible for making JLF click. Is it the Jaipur Virasat Foundation that gave birth to the concept of Jaipur Literature Festival? Or is it Teamwork Arts, the company that has put things in order to work out a successful formula? Or is it Sanjoy Roy, the producer of JLF and the man behind Teamwork Arts, or the Festival Directors Namita Gokhale and William Dalrymple?

Others consider the fact that the Diggi family has also made it possible for JLF to grow in stature and prestige. Some even feel that the credit of the lit fest's success should go to the book lovers who have come out in increasing numbers to make the lit fest what it is now.

A few people give credit to the January atmosphere of Jaipur when it's perhaps the most happening place in this continent. The Pink City's touristic aura can't be dismissed either for attracting visitors to this literature festival.

Another fact is that, given the scale and size of the lit fest, it is impossible to pull off an event of such proportions without the active support of the government administration, police, civic bodies etc.

As we observe the completion of the historic 10-year celebrations of Jaipur Literature Festival, volunteers must be seen as an integral part of the festival. JLF is well-known for bringing together people from across social and economic divides. Volunteers are the 'eyes' of the festival and more so in terms of security. Each volunteer is specially trained before the festival begins, ready to face any eventuality.

This year, the festival welcomes about 300 volunteers, all divided into various departments such as logistics, venue management, technical, social media, registrations, and others. Each department has its own manager, whom the volunteers report to for carrying out their daily duties.

JLF encourages its 'eyes' to not only be the watchdogs of the festival but also enjoy the event, bonding with their group members. The volunteers are adept at maintaining their cool and remaining focused and cantered when dealing with disrespectful guests. Volunteers have come from all over the country and some even from abroad. The majority of them are from Jaipur, Mumbai and Delhi.

Each volunteer is an advocate of the values of the festival, receiving all guests with a respectful Namaste and grace. Let us all salute these unsung volunteers who put service above self to ensure that the lit fest takes place smoothly. Aren't these volunteers the ones who make this festival click?

Lit Nama, *DNA*, Jaipur

January 22, 2017

75

Rajasthani Flavour of JLF

In the past, there have been allegations that JLF promotes mainly English literature and has very few well-known Hindi writers. Although Rajasthani sessions have been included, many Rajasthani authors stay away from JLF.

Though a literature festival, JLF is also a potpourri of many things cultural and fashionable. A stronger presence of local litterateurs would only add to its exceptional ambience.

But a few local authors allege that JLF invites only one lobby of authors each year. Likewise, apart from some folk singers at the dinners, Rajasthani performing artists, music and dance are missing from JLF. After these concerns were raised from various quarters at the state level, some welcome changes were made and instrumentalist Vishwa Mohan Bhatt performed at JLF.

This year, too, the evening music programme line-up at the Clarks Amer presented a great variety. However, many feel that the traditional Rajasthani element should be given wider representation.

In JLF's 10th year, Rajasthani elements blended in well at the festival venue — Diggi Palace, itself a haveli-turned-heritage hotel. For many days before the fest, workers were engaged to transform the palace into a venue for hosting the literary 'Kumbh Mela' of Jaipur.

Stalls for authors to sign books are invariably set up near all major tents. This year, these stalls were either decorated with cut-outs of moustaches or a large papier-mâché peacock — both in typical Rajasthani style. The sides of various tents were done up with dangling square cloths adorned with motifs of peacocks, camels, trees, huts, etc. Bright and colourful Rajasthani paisley-printed yellow tents were set up in front of Durbar Hall surrounding the fountain.

People mingled around the stalls behind the Mughal Tent selling traditional bric-a-brac amid a fusion of Rajasthani desert music, books on Rajasthan, a wide array of colourful stoles, printed bags, journals, plush toys, pouches and elephant, camel and tiger-printed *kurtis* for men and women. At the walkway to Diggi, colourful puppets were on sale.

The Delegate Lunch area got pretty crowded as people stood in queues waiting to taste items like *bajre ka churma*, which are part of a typical Rajasthani meal. We hope, in the coming years, more state artistes get to perform at JLF, and more importantly, authors from all the regions come here and add to the pageantry.

Lit Nama, DNA, Jaipur

January 23, 2017

76

Brand JLF and Literary Tourism

With Jaipur Literature Festival (JLF) drawing to a close, the Pink City completed a decade of 'literary tourism'.

The city, at this time, faces a rush of domestic and international tourists who are here to attend JLF. The five-day festival hosts prominent writers, historians, poets, translators and editors, in addition to more than a million book lovers from around the world. Their presence also revs up the local economy and helps many hotels, food joints, tour operators, and shops. No wonder all hotels are booked months in advance, flight prices double and trains, buses, and vehicles on rent are all jam-packed.

Restaurants and food joints are also in demand during the lit fest. What is pleasantly surprising is that demonetisation does not seem to have had an adverse impact on the festival, apart from some temporary chaos at the cashless counters that was more technical in nature.

Economically, the mega literary event makes huge business sense for tour operators. They have added JLF to their itinerary to woo national and international clients and curated their tour packages in such a manner that visitors to the city get a feel of JLF, which is now an important element of the city's tourism calendar.

Chief Minister Vasundhara Raje, herself a book lover, has said on many occasions that JLF is a big-time branding exercise for Jaipur. The name of Jaipur has been marketed well in the USA, the UK and even South Africa. This year, there is a plan to popularise Jaipur and the fest in Australia, too.

The festival has done a remarkable job by including Amber Fort and Hawa Mahal as evening venues. These places are showcased to tourists and Jaipurites.

Jaipur is widely known for the shopping experience it offers. Places like Johari Bazaar, Bapu Bazaar and Nehru Bazaar are flooded with avid bargain-hunters. Tourists take time out from books to indulge in shopping for ethnic attire, exquisite handicrafts, traditional puppets and bric-a-brac.

Therefore, along with medical tourism, heritage tourism, wedding destination or honeymoon tourism, and film location tourism, a new addition is 'literary tourism', as people have started travelling for literature festivals as well.

JLF, in the past decade, has triggered several such literary festivals in other cities of India that has resulted in a significant boom in tourism. It would, therefore, be apt to say that JLF is truly the father of literary tourism in the country.

Lit Nama, DNA, Jaipur

January 24, 2017

77

Star Power, Politics and a Surprise Addition

Jaipur Literature Festival has just ended on a high note. Like every year, it attracted scores of people but had its own set of glitches and controversies, too.

JLF went cashless this year to streamline transactions throughout the festival. As per the cashless system, each visitor's festival pass had a unique QR code which was scanned every day at the entry and exit points. The guests were intimated of this in advance. By visiting one of the cashless counters at the festival, one could put money into the cards and make transactions with various vendors at the festival.

However, on the first day, visitors faced difficulty in adding money into their respective passes and were compelled to use cash. Similarly, vendors who sold almost half of their stocks, were surprised to see no money in their account. Clearly, there had been a glitch.

The festival, celebrating the theme 'The Freedom to Dream: India at 70', was inaugurated by Chief Minister of Rajasthan Vasundhara Raje, Man Booker Prize winner Paul Beatty, much-admired lyricist Gulzar, American poet Anne Waldman and mystic yogi and guru Sadhguru Jaggi Vasudev. At the time of the lamp-lighting ceremony, fireworks went off in front of the stage. Media personnel, unaware of the display, faced difficulty in retreating quickly and a few of them got mild burns.

Days before the festival began, controversies started building up around a talk featuring Manmohan Vaidya, the head of the RSS's communications department, and Dattatreya Hosabale, a joint general secretary of the RSS. Newspapers reported that CPIM leaders would stay away from the festival.

Taslima Nasreen's session, which wasn't announced earlier, except for the word 'Exile' on the schedule, was preponed to noon from 3.45pm. People at the Front Lawn were surprised to see her walking up on stage for the session. Even the media was surprised. Later, some Muslim protesters came to raise an objection to her session, but the matter was sorted out in a closed-door meeting at Hotel White Lily.

The festival had something for everybody, from films to fiction, mythology and history to economy and global affairs. The festival chaired a packed session on Brexit — the most divisive issue in Britain right now — with A.N. Wilson, Andrew Roberts, Linda Colley, Surjit Bhalla and Timothy Garton Ash in conversation with Jonathan Shainin.

Amitabh Kant, the CEO of Niti Aayog, in his session, 'Brave New World: The Virtual Economy and Beyond', questioned the need for demonetisation, the push towards a digital economy, disruptive policies, and a need for the right internet infrastructure and faster processes to enable people to set up bank accounts. People also got to see one of India's most famous film stars, Rishi Kapoor, who discussed his new book, *Khullam Khulla,* with his fans.

sundeepbhutoria.blogspot.com

January 25, 2017

78

January in Jaipur

January means Jaipur... literature, art, culture, sports and whatnot, and above all, ZEE Jaipur Literature Festival. January is the best season to be in Jaipur. There is a flurry of activity, a compelling conglomeration of creativity.

One of the January gifts presented every year not only to Jaipur but to the whole creative community is ZEE Jaipur Literature Festival, or in keeping with the current times — nice and short — JLF (Even the Parallel Literature Festival named themselves PLF). The graph of Jaipur lit fest continues to grow steadily upwards. Diggi Palace bustles with the excitement and joy of multitudes of people thronging ZEE JLF every year.

Several events happen in January and increase in magnitude around these five days of ZEE JLF — the world's largest free literature festival, as the organisers say. But many say that it's also the most commercialised literature festival.

This time ZEE JLF visitors will have the opportunity

to visit contemporary architecture exhibitions, lifestyle exhibitions as well as club and cafe openings in the city. People can begin the year with gusto — attending events, parties, festivals and catching up with one's long-lost friends and, of course, polo.

One can never have enough of the culture and festivities in Jaipur. The icing on the cake is the Rajasthani cuisine that the gastronomically inclined will never tire of. Not just the fabled *dal baati churma* but a cuisine that can boast of rich, aromatic royal dishes as well as the simple, humble but unique foods that linger on the palate for hours. This is especially applicable to those who love to lick their fingers after finishing a meal. (For those who really wish to have a quick bite, go to Tapri).

This time during ZEE Jaipur Literature Festival, the audience will get a special treat. January has gifted the people of Jaipur with a jewellery museum. Amrapali Museum, the first of its kind, has opened its gates in the Pink City. The museum has been conceptualised by Rajiv Arora and Rajesh Ajmera and curated by my friend, Pramod KG.

The museum showcases the traditional silver jewelled arts of India, reflecting the 'everyday life' of the people of Rajasthan. The exhibits at Amrapali Museum are profoundly different, both in their nature and in the way they have been collected. Amrapali Museum will also be of immense help to scholars, students, connoisseurs and other visitors to Jaipur, who will get to explore the heritage and history of India through its jewellery and artefacts. The rich and varied culture of the state is manifested in the objects displayed here.

Lit Nama, DNA, Jaipur

January 24, 2018

79

Of Sessions and Discussions

At ZEE JLF, there is an event called JLF Bookmark (JBM), which started in 2014. JLF is not just a place for authors but is *the* place to be seen for all creative people. JBM has evolved into a forum that brings together publishers, literary agents, writers, translators and booksellers to 'talk shop' through focused sessions and roundtable discussions. I was invited to be a part of the roundtable as well, but I won't be able to because of a prior engagement.

Bookmark also hosts stimulating discussions with aspiring writers, literary agents and publishers, book cover designers, graphic artists and audio and digital platform providers. As a part of JBM, *The First Book Club New Writers Mentorship Programme* was held for the second time this year. The programme saw entries ranging from short stories and poetry to works of fiction and non-fiction by first-time writers across the country.

Just before JLF began, I visited Jawahar Kala Kendra (JKK). My visit there had been long overdue. It was created to preserve and promote various genres of Indian art and culture in 1991 and is supposed to act as a facilitator for art connoisseurs, scholars, artists and artisans to interact with one another.

JKK was designed by Charles Correa, one of the best-known architects of our country. The architecture of JKK is based on the concept of Indian astrology and resembles the original plan of Jaipur, with nine squares. The building of the institution represents the nine planets, making it quite unique. Each section represents the characteristics of one planet. The library, for instance, is located in the Jupiter section, which symbolises knowledge and wisdom. The murals from Jain mythology, the charts and paintings on the ceiling of the central dome, attract tourists and artists. Throughout the year, there are seminars, workshops, dance and music recitals, theatre performances and publication of books on art and culture.

The other day, I saw six exhibition halls and felt proud of this place that could compete with the best of art and cultural institutions in the world. At the same time, it is deeply entrenched in the Rajasthani soil. An example is the Shilpagram — a rural complex of six huts — each of which represents the different regions of Rajasthan. We owe our gratitude to Pooja Sood, director-general of JKK, who has not only revamped the place but breathed a new life into its walls.

My belief is that one cannot be global without first being local; at the same time, to promote local performing arts you have to have a global vision. My request to my friend Sanjoy Roy is that next year some sessions of JLF or performing art activities should be held here at the JKK. JKK being a popular cultural destination and ZEE JLF being an established brand could probably come together to host a few sessions, especially the ones pertaining to Rajasthani literature. That would be welcomed by everybody.

Lit Nama, *DNA*, Jaipur

January 25, 2018

80

Who Created JLF?

When I think of ZEE Jaipur Literature Festival, I cannot help thinking that this is *the* place that takes the credit for holding the greatest literary show on earth. One knows that in the earlier days, art and culture flourished under the patronage of royal families. That the Pink City, with such a vibrant culture and regal splendour, should be the creator of such a festival is hardly surprising.

However, what is surprising is the stature JLF has attained in these few years. An initiative of Jaipur Virasat Foundation, the festival is endearingly referred to as the 'Kumbh of literature festivals'. Every year, the festival brings together a diverse mix of the world's greatest writers, thinkers, humanitarians, politicians, business leaders, sports people and entertainers on one stage.

Till date, more than 2,000 speakers have attended JLF. Past speakers include Nobel laureates like Orhan Pamuk, J.M. Coetzee and Wole Soynika, and our very own Sahitya Akademi winners like Girish Karnad, Gulzar, Javed Akhtar,

M.T. Vasudevan Nair and the late Mahasweta Devi, among others. The list of illustrious personalities not only includes modern literary names like Amish Tripathi and Vikram Seth but stalwarts like Amartya Sen, Amitabh Bachchan, A.P.J. Abdul Kalam, Oprah Winfrey and the Dalai Lama, too.

Sometimes I wonder, what is it that makes JLF, JLF? I have been a witness to ZEE JLF since its inception and the way it has grown and transcended Indian borders has made it an impressive brand. So, what is so special about JLF?

Is it the venue of Diggi Palace? Is it the beautiful January weather? Is it the touristy charm of Jaipur? Is it the greeting style of Ram Pratap Singh Diggi? Is it the famous Diggi Puri tea? Is it the instinct for controversy, from Salman Rushdie to Prasoon Joshi? Is it the Bollywood enchantment? Is it the single malt parties held in plush surroundings of luxurious hotels? Is it the sessions curated by festival director William Dalrymple? Is it Teamwork Arts' global networking skills? Is it the lure of *dal baati churma*? Or is it the ability of the government and police administration?

The answer to all the above questions is YES and NO. All of the above have contributed to JLF, no doubt, but I personally feel that the backbone of JLF is its team of volunteers. As I wrote last year also, the commitment and spirit of the team of boys and girls led by Sanjoy Roy of Teamwork Arts is the biggest reason behind making JLF what it is today.

A few years ago, I was a witness to the sudden rains leading to the collapse of the lawn venue when Sanjoy Roy and his team assembled at 4am to begin shifting the venues to the halls of Diggi Palace, instead of cancelling the event. It left me completely dumbfounded — the sheer dedication and team spirit of all the volunteers.

This column is dedicated to these volunteers with a never-say-die attitude. Let us all cheer out loud for them and salute them this Republic Day!

Lit Nama, DNA, Jaipur

January 26, 2018

81

A Method in the Madness

No Gulzar, Javed Akhtar, or the evergreen Suhel Seth this year, and while I am writing this, I read that Prasoon Joshi will also not be a part of ZEE JLF this time round. The absence of these three stalwarts affects the presence of Hindi poetry and songs this year, but does it affect the crowd?

When the literature festival got underway in 2006, it was a humble beginning with the Durbar Hall and two other venues in the front. The now-fabled Front Lawn and Samvad didn't make their appearance back then. As the festival continued to grow exponentially, more venues were added to accommodate the massive number of people pouring in on a daily basis.

Recently, Samvad has been shifted outside Diggi Palace to near the main road, right after Lord's Hotel. Other than that, the musical maestros of JLF have been known to perform on all four nights of the festival.

The musical magic was created earlier in Diggi

Palace itself, but as the festival grew, the artistes began descending upon the exclusive venue of Clarks Amer to give the audience a glimpse of their musical extravaganza. Heritage evenings are also a part of the festival; these are held in the iconic venues of Hawa Mahal and Amber Fort. The exquisite background provided by these monuments proves to be the perfect venue for musical performances, which encapsulate the soul of Rajasthan.

The way the festival is gaining momentum, it is inevitable that it will grow even more and expand to uncover newer venues. Whenever a celebrity enters the festival, a swarm of people rushes in like angry bees, each struggling to find its little corner of respite to attend the beloved celebrity's session.

The same was the case on Friday as people's favourite Nawazuddin Siddiqui came to address the session, *Manto: The man and the legend,* with Bollywood actress-director and friend Nandita Das.

There was no place to stand and vast crowds had covered Diggi Palace as far as the eye could see. At one point, the number of people increased so much that visitors could neither enter the venue nor go out.

And yet, somehow, year after year, JLF still manages to find a method in the madness. Such is the true spirit of JLF. Despite the huge volumes of people, JLF makes sure to follow all security protocols. The festival organisers and volunteers guide and safely move people out of the aisles to facilitate smooth entry and exit so that a situation of emergency never comes to pass.

There have been talks of shifting JLF from Diggi Palace, but you cannot get the same taste of tea anywhere else, anywhere apart from Gulabji tea stall! You cannot have Jaipur weather in Assam, you cannot have the pleasure of *dal baati churma* in big fat celebrations overseas.

The same way, without Diggi Palace's ambience, you cannot have JLF; maybe a few things here and there can be shifted, but not the whole festival.

Lit Nama, DNA, Jaipur

January 28, 2018

82

ZEE JLF sans nom Jaipur

Would Jaipur Literature Festival (JLF) be the same if the name Jaipur wasn't a part of it?

ZEE Jaipur Literature Festival is one of the world's largest and most-awaited festivals in the world, held each year in the Pink City. Besides book lovers and litterateurs, the festival is a jamboree for the selfie brigade and fashionistas, who put their best foot forward to show off their latest bags, sunglasses and collectibles. Also, there are those who are there because they wish to be seen as belonging to the fraternity of literature lovers and intellectuals.

I have wondered what would have been the status of ZEE Jaipur lit fest if the name Jaipur wasn't a part of it. I think that JLF would have lost its magic without Jaipur being a part of its name. After all, when JLF is held in cities like London and Boulder in Colorado, it evokes a very typical imagery that is steeped in the history and culture of Rajasthan and the name Jaipur.

So, it makes sense to have Jaipur as a part of the festival's name. The Pink City has much to offer — one of the best tourist spots of India, rich colourful heritage, music, dance, history, cultural pageantry and tradition. So, while the festival has given much to Jaipur in terms of audience, business and recognition, it has also leveraged the enchanting effects of the city through the ambience of Jaipur as well as a sense of belonging that is peculiar to this place.

While Rajasthan is still fighting to get an official status in the Constitution of India for the Rajasthani language, JLF has helped promote Rajasthani outside India in a big way. I, however, think JLF still owes much to Jaipur and should pay some kind of a tribute or royalty to the Pink City. Not in a strictly monetary sense, but something a la a GI tag.

GI or Geographical Indication is a sign used on products that have a specific geographical origin and possess qualities or a reputation that are due to that origin. In order to function as a GI, a sign must identify a product as originating in a given place.

Had JLF engaged more local intellectuals and given them the respect extended to others, the festival would have become more representative in nature. Had it been so, all those who are linked to the literary sphere would have empathised with the festival and the question of holding competing festivals wouldn't have popped up.

No one can deny the fact that JLF has contributed much towards changing the economic landscape of the city; generating business and setting cash registers ringing. But at the end of the day, money isn't everything, my friend.

Lit Nama, DNA, Jaipur

January 29, 2018

83

Salute to Jaipur Police

At ZEE JLF each year, we are amazed to witness Diggi Palace accommodating increasing crowds from session to session. At last, Samvad had to be shifted outside the venue this year.

We all owe a big 'thank you' to Jaipur Police for working tirelessly 24x7 to manage crowds and ensure the smooth functioning of the festival. The police are always very attentive and prevent controversies from snowballing into a law-and-order problem.

The police of Jaipur during the lit fest days remind me of Kolkata Police during the Durga Puja festivities, who are on duty for extended periods, sacrificing their holidays and sleep to keep things in order. Like their counterparts in the City of Joy, Jaipur Police also work beyond their call of duty, with individual policemen and policewomen always putting their service above the self. My associate in Jaipur, Apra Kuchhal, told me that the Jaipur Police Commissioner personally makes rounds of the festival venue time and again.

I think we all agree that ZEE Jaipur Literature Festival also owes its current reputation to popular support. It is high time the people should know about the selection process of the authors at the festival. Something which belongs to the people should be transparent and known to the public as well.

Many a time, allegations have been raised against the process of selecting authors. It is rumoured that the selection is based on the whims and fancies of individuals. Also, those who are not in the good books of the organisers are believed to have little chance of participating officially.

Though the festival organisers claim that the speakers and sessions are fixed well in advance, it is a known fact that there are many last-minute entries. As an organiser of a small literary series called Kalam, which stands nowhere in comparison with ZEE JLF, we have a presence in about 14 cities in India and also abroad and expect to reach out to 25 cities across India soon.

Even for a small event like Kalam, when it comes to the selection of our authors, all our stakeholders have an equal say in the selection process. In fact, many times it has so happened that the authors we selected were rejected by our partners. This has added more strength and respect to the entire process and been much appreciated by the other stakeholders of Kalam.

Maybe, I am not adequately aware of the selection process of the world's biggest free literature festival. But if ZEE JLF adheres to due process, we must appreciate it. And if the same is made known to the public, it would be admirable.

Lit Nama, DNA, Jaipur

January 30, 2018

84

All's Well that Ends Well

Things couldn't have ended on a better note for Jaipur Literature Festival — thanks to Prasoon Joshi. The five-day festival is like a home for authors, poets, lyricists, actors, historians, journalists and many more brilliant minds. The festival is all about literature and, of course, fashion and star hotel single malt parties.

ZEE JLF continued being a cashless festival for the second year in a row. Visitors used plastic cards throughout the festival for payments. The cards could be used at food stalls and the festival bazaar. By visiting one of the cashless counters at the festival one could add money to the cards and carry out transactions at the festival with various vendors.

This streamlined system was also seen in the visitor's festival pass, which had a unique QR code to be scanned every day at the entry and exit points.

The 11th ZEE Jaipur Literature Festival kicked off on January 25 with energetic music from Gujarat, Assam and Rajasthan. The festival was inaugurated by Former Rajasthan Governor Margaret Alva and British-born American essayist and novelist Pico Iyer. He also delivered the keynote address on this occasion.

Poetry was a dominant theme at this year's JLF, as were sessions on woman-centric writing. Modern poets like Rupi Kaur held the audience in a trance as she performed poetry from her books, *Milk & Honey* and *The Sun and her Flowers*. People clicked their fingers, as is the norm in a poetry slam, to show their appreciation for Rupi's beautiful poetry.

The festival also kept its promise to provide visitors with the perfect mix of star power, mythology, history, economics and more. The festival chaired a packed session on the *Magical Mystery Tour: The Beatles in India* with Philip Norman in conversation with Ajoy Bose. In the session *In a Life in Music,* tabla maestro Zakir Hussain spoke of his dedication and love for the tabla. He also shared his experiences and memories of working with other legends of the music industry.

Other than this, popular actress Soha Ali Khan attracted a large crowd in her session, *The Perils of Celebrity* with the legendary Sharmila Tagore, who also happens to be her mother.

But the showstopper was certainly the session *Manto:*

The Man and the Legend with actress-director Nandita Das and actor Nawazuddin Siddiqui. This popular session witnessed never-ending crowds covering Diggi Palace. With the inevitable question of censorship popping up from the audience, a negative outlook was reflected by the panel on aggressive groups adopting the role of people's guardians in today's society.

JLF and controversies have always been known to go hand-in-hand. This time was no different as controversies around *Padmaavat* dominated the event. A few of the sessions discussed the controversial film briefly. As threats of the Karni Sena continued to loom over CBFC chief Prasoon Joshi, people were left to wonder whether he'd be coming or not. The curiosity finally ended on January 27 with an official statement from Joshi that he would not be attending the festival.

The crowds did get a little thinner as the festival drew to a close, but interesting sessions kept many coming back for more. Besides the celebrations within Diggi Palace, cultural performances were held at the beautiful monuments, Amber Fort and Hawa Mahal.

The city of Jaipur is sad to bid farewell to this roller-coaster ride of art and artistic freedom that has motored along for the past five days. But the city is also hopeful and excited to see what ZEE JLF will bring next year. As we say in Bengal — "*Aschhe bochhor abaar hobe*" (Until next year).

Lit Nama, DNA, Jaipur

January 31, 2018

85

The Grandest Lit Fest

The 12th Edition of ZEE Jaipur Literature Festival is taking place this year with a new local government in place, set to be one of the biggest events in its history in terms of scale and magnitude.

In a freewheeling session of Prabha Khaitan Foundation's 'Ek Mulakat' on Tuesday, Sanjoy Roy, the managing director of Teamwork Arts and the man behind JLF, shared aspects of the lit fest not known to many. The volume of business that JLF brings to the state is mind-boggling. This year, as informed by Mr Roy, nearly 600 media persons have been given accreditation from India and across the world. A few years ago, for the first time, an economic survey was done and it was estimated that JLF contributed nearly Rs 30 crore to the local economy. Last year, Ernst & Young did a basic survey in which they included commerce in jewellery, furniture, clothing, home products, restaurants and hotels and the figure was Rs 116 crore. The scale of the lit fest's contribution to the local economy can be gauged from the fact that bookstores sell over about 100,000 books, valued in crores, during JLF.

There is speculation in many quarters that Diggi Palace is not big enough for hosting the fest. Roy, however, feels that there is no other venue in Jaipur that provides such ambience and infrastructure to host the festival. He had scouted around for a 'better venue', but the ones he visited did not come close to Diggi Palace. The fact that there are nearly 125 washrooms to cater to the crowds is an indicator towards the kind of logistics JLF demands. Other logistical details are no less eye-popping.

Also, JLF has to factor in numerous new issues every year. For example, the local health department team keeps doctors, staff, medicines and ambulances ready to screen people for influenza-like illness (ILI) and provide masks and medicines to those who show symptoms.

This year, writer-historian William Dalrymple would be conspicuous by his absence. He had tweeted his apologies on January 16 saying that following the death of his father, Sir Hew Fleetwood Hamilton-Dalrymple, he would not be able to attend. William was very active during the Mumbai curtain-raiser for the lit fest in December 2018.

The lit fest has a formidable line-up of 350 speakers, cutting across fields and genres, including Nobel Prize-winning structural biologist Venkatraman Ramakrishnan (author of *Gene Machine*), Pulitzer Award-winning heavyweight authors, feminist writers, Dalit writers and so on, covering 16 Indian and 12 international languages. This is perhaps what makes JLF 'the grandest lit fest in the world'.

Over the years, I have witnessed the stupendous growth of Jaipur lit fest. The acorn has become a mighty oak.

I think Jaipur lit fest is like a salad-bowl where authors, writers, politicians, foreign visitors, bureaucrats, actors, activists, artists, book lovers and local residents come together for five days — each retaining their unique identities like different ingredients in a salad bowl — to celebrate the pulsating spirit of the Pink City.

Moreover, Jaipur's culture and tradition blend into it. I was pleasantly surprised to see Javed Akhtar, Shashi Tharoor, Devdutt Pattanaik and even Lord Jeffery Archer enjoying wearing the turban at my get-together at ITC Rajputana. What more do we want?

Lit Nama, *DNA*, Jaipur

January 24, 2019

86

The Lit Evening is Back!

The Maha Kumbh of literature, ZEE Jaipur Literature Festival 2019, got off to a gala start with a traditional dinner at Taj Rambagh Palace. The equestrian and polo-themed stable bric-a-brac showed the effort put into the décor. This is one evening that is meticulously hosted, covering the minute detail of aesthetic, décor and food in order to revive the regal aura of a bygone era.

The closed-door dinner at Rambagh was started with the objective of getting authors and writers to meet one another on the eve of the lit fest. But over the years, a steady influx of bureaucrats, corporate executives and Jaipurites has vastly outnumbered the presence of authors. So much so that making it to this dinner had become a prestige issue for many, who do not hesitate to pull strings to get their names on the guest list. Thus, it has become a crowded affair and belittled the basic purpose of hosting all the guest authors so they can meet one another ahead of the literary carnival.

A few years ago, I had been present with the celeb authors at this prestigious dinner. Many authors, I noticed, started eating dinner in the privacy of their rooms. I am glad that from this year onwards, the Rambagh dinner is back on track with most authors and litterateurs attending it rather than choosing to isolate in their rooms.

There has been a much-needed course correction in the guest list and due weightage given to the presence of authors. This year only select Jaipurites and prominent media persons received invitations. There are many people I got to meet exclusively at this dinner, such as Rajkumar Vijit Singh. I must say it was a fantastic mix of authors, JLF guests and key persons of Jaipur. I must also congratulate the organisers for taking positive steps to revive the stature of the Rambagh dinner, and I hope that this year's arrangements lay down a precedent of sorts, putting to rest the clamour for getting onto the coveted guest list.

On a different note, the polo-inspired theme added, in the right measure, an aura of royal Rajasthani heritage to the 184-year-old iconic property, which had been the abode of Maharajas and Maharanis and also served as a hunting lodge. Before the Rambagh Palace dinner, I had gone to the Diggi Palace hotel, which too is a heritage property. There, I met poet Chandra Prakash Deval, author

Kishwar Desai and publishers Urvashi Butalia and Neeta Gupta, among others.

I must thank Thakur Rampratap Singh Diggi for showing me around the new venue at Diggi Palace. I did get a feel of the massive infrastructural arrangements that have been put in place for the smooth operations of the lit fest.

The very success of JLF hinges on robust infrastructure and back-office support. Diggi Palace has been the venue of JLF since it took off in 2006. Having witnessed the festival's stupendous growth, it still presents, for me, the best option as a prime venue.

Lit Nama, DNA, Jaipur

January 25, 2019

87

When Authors Let their Hair Down

JLF does not just mean an invigorating literary dialogue and engagement, it also involves a number of interesting parties that are held on the sidelines of the main event. Over the years, besides the mega event at Diggi Palace and the Music Stage at Clarks Amer, publishers also host their own bashes.

This year, closed-door events were hosted by Westland, Rupa, Aleph and Pan Macmillan for their respective authors and teams. The idea is to interact closely with associates in a cosy atmosphere.

On Thursday evening, the cocktails at Rambagh, organised by HarperCollins, and the one at ITC Rajputana, where my team and associates interacted with authors from Westland, saw quite a gathering. The latter saw a violinist from Jaipur playing Hindi movie numbers in the background. Film star Shatrughan Sinha, poet Javed Akhtar, actor and writer Shabana Azmi, author Devdutt Pattanaik, author and politician Pavan K. Varma, novelists Anita Nair and Savi Sharma and others interacted with our associates.

The guests had a whale of a time with a variety of spirited drinks, sumptuous food and dulcet music. One special feature of the evening was that each male guest had been adorned with a turban for a special ethnic touch.

On Friday, it was Jeffery Archer and other authors from Pan Macmillan, besides closed-door events with Rupa and Aleph authors.

January always means a rich mix of art, culture, literature, polo and much more. The pleasant weather complements the aura of the Pink City. To celebrate this spirit, a special event, 'January of Jaipur', has been curated. It is an evening of warm conversations about all things Jaipur in the month of January.

There was, however, an unfortunate incident involving the branch of a tree falling on some people in the restricted delegate area. The injured were given medical aid and taken to the hospital and discharged after treatment.

On the other hand, the unexpected rain could not mar the spirit of the festival and the sessions ran on schedule. The organisers have learnt from the 2014 showers and are now better equipped to handle the vagaries of the weather.

Lit Nama, DNA, Jaipur

January 26, 2019

88

A City of Literature?

Home to one of world's largest free literary fests, Jaipur does not feature in the UNESCO-designated list of City of Literature. Currently, 28 cities from 23 countries have been given the tag 'City of Literature' by UNESCO. While cities of smaller nations like Estonia, Slovenia and Uruguay are on the list, there isn't a single city from India. Even the war-ravaged Iraqi capital of Baghdad made it to this coveted list in 2015.

There is some consolation, though, that Jaipur is the sole Indian city, among 179 others, to feature in the category of 'Creative Cities of Craft and Folk Art' under the UNESCO Creative Cities Network (UCCN) programme.

I strongly feel that Jaipur and Kolkata — being the country's cultural and literary capitals respectively — are the two Indian cities that can qualify for the UNESCO list. Kolkata is gearing up to meet the criteria and stake its claim. Edinburgh Napier University, which contributed much to help the city of Edinburgh become the first UNdesignated 'City of Literature', is keen to help Kolkata get on that list. A dynamic Indian lady and author, Jai Verma, who helped Nottingham become a UNESCO City of Literature in 2015, is also campaigning for Kolkata. Jaipur too should buck up and submit its bid to the UN in earnest.

Why a UNESCO tag?

Many may wonder if the juice is worth the squeeze! I think so. I feel that JLF should use its stature and appeal to promote literary creativity in Rajasthan and should not be viewed just as a world-class literary jamboree. The Pink City should also look beyond the scenic celebration of the written word and create new infrastructure to expand the literary and cultural capital base. Sadly, no serious effort has been made to approach the UN so far.

The UNESCO recognition, which is based on several criteria, would go a long way to confirm Jaipur's cultural and literary heritage and boost creativity and local language literature. Also, there is much to gain by being a part of a global UN initiative that brings together 1,000 libraries, 70 lit fests and 900 bookshops.

Each city and lit fest have its own cachet. In contrast to JLF, The Hay Festival of Literature and Arts in Wales takes place in a town with a population of 1,600 people and 28 bookstores. However, during the 10-day festival, the town's population multiplies astonishingly to somewhere around 2,50,000.

The famous Edinburgh International Book Festival has the only rail station in the world — Waverley Station — named after a book, written by Sir Walter Scott. Small towns and cities have made a big contribution to literary activities to become a part of a global UN network.

On the other hand, cities like Jaipur, Brooklyn, Tokyo, Sydney, Mandalay and others hosting famous lit fests aren't on the UNESCO list, which recognises only those cities that place creativity and cultural industries at the heart of their development plans.

Lit Nama, DNA, Jaipur

January 28, 2019

89

A Twitter Bee in the JLF Bonnet

The increasingly popular Twitter handle *@JLFInsider* that comes alive during Jaipur Literature Festival is like a bee in the JLF bonnet. It gratifies our yearning for masala by tweeting gossip, faux pas, trivia and facts wrapped in sensationalism and satire. And it does a good job of it by being anonymous and crowdsourcing live tweets that have a ring of truth. Like citizen journalists, we now have 'citizen Twitteratis' who help keep the handle's curiosity quotient high.

With 7,180 followers and counting, *@JLFInsider* is like chilli flakes. For many, it adds to the taste. But it is too hot for others. Either way, it has become one of the most engaging voices of JLF since its arrival in 2014.

This Twitter handle reminds me of the controversial anonymous blog called Fake IPL Player, which was started in 2009 coinciding with the IPL tournament. By narrating sordid stories and giving uncanny names to players, coaches and team owners, the popularity of the blog shot through the roof. Everyone started guessing about the person behind the blog. All this was put to rest when a marketing specialist called Anupam Mukerji, who had never met a cricketer in his life, revealed himself on television and to newspapers as the person writing the blog by making up stories.

I remember many bureaucrats used to bookmark and follow a website called *whispersinthecorridors* when it started. Many of them said that it doled out inside information that turned out to be true. The initial anonymity added to the site's credibility.

In the same vein, people are trying to guess who runs *@JLFInsider* on Twitter. Of course, journalists, public relations outfits, authors and disgruntled members of the JLF management team are the ones whose names naturally come up first. But the concept of crowdsourcing seems more plausible.

The 'Insider' is certainly fond of sarcasm. For instance, the tweets from Manisha Koirala's session — *Healed: Life Learnings from Manisha Koirala* — poked fun at her alcoholic proclivities.

At times, images with funny captions by Twitter users are put up. Some people think *@JLFInsider* is the bold voice of the people and their activities at the festival. They could be standing behind you, attending sessions, sipping wine at the bar or trying to be within earshot in the unlikeliest of places as citizen Twitterati.

A few of my author friends have asked me, are you the one behind *@JLFInsider*? No way, me, the techno handicap? Yet, others think it is a PR person with his team stationed at Diggi Palace or perhaps someone close to (organiser) Sanjoy Roy's team. Few also point out that it may be a publicity gimmick from the organisers themselves, which I don't believe.

On a serious note, the world has seen the Snowden effect and encouraged many to become whistle-blowers and insiders. How does it matter who is behind *@JLFInsider* as long as what they tweet isn't libellous? The mainstream media is, by and large, subservient to the ads they receive. Let social media have its say. We should take it all in our stride.

Let me share another fact — the organisers' move to stop online registrations during the holidays on January 26 and 27 has helped manage the crowds and spared the lit fest the maddening rush of visitors. From a security perspective, too, it was a step in the right direction.

Lit Nama, DNA, Jaipur

January 29, 2019

ABOUT THE AUTHOR

Sundeep Bhutoria is a social activist working in the field of social welfare, international cultural cooperation and the promotion of Indian arts. Born in Rajasthan, Sundeep is based in Kolkata, and under normal circumstances, travels every week.

Through his various NGOs, he helps carry out different kinds of cultural activities with the aim of preserving and promoting India's rich cultural heritage. Some of the programmes he has been instrumental in instituting and executing are An Author's Afternoon, Aakhar, Chaupal, Desert Soul, Desert Storm, Ek Mulakat, Kalam, Karuna, Lafz, Recipe Rendezvous, Sanskar, Tete-a-Tea, The Write Circle, The Universe Writes etc.

He also runs various projects for women, children and the elderly, one of which is Pronam — run in collaboration with Kolkata Police — an outreach programme for the welfare of elderly citizens.

He serves as a Member of the Expert Committee of

Cultural Function and Production Grant of the Ministry of Culture, Government of India, and as a member of the Advisory Committee of the Indian Council for Cultural Relations (ICCR). He is also the Treasurer of the World Federation of United Nations Associations (WFUNA).

In September 2010, he was felicitated at The House of Lords, London, for excellence in his chosen fields of work.

Sundeep has authored six other books till date. His first book in English, *The Safari*, centres around wildlife preservation and tiger protection in India, while his first book in Hindi chronicles his experiences in different countries, titled *Aap Biti Jag Biti*. His second book in English, *My Life My Travels*, a travelogue that touches upon the cultural and social mores in different countries, gleaned through his own experiences, became a bestseller. His third book, *China Diary*, is a travelogue published by Pan Macmillan in November 2019. He then published *Calcuttascape: Musings of a Globetrotter* in July 2020, and followed it with *Bera Bond*, on the leopards of Bera in Rajasthan. He is currently working on two other books on his travels.

Sundeep lives in Kolkata with his wife Manjari and daughter Aavya, and divides his time across Kolkata, Delhi, Rajasthan and London.

Also by Sundeep Bhutoria

English

The Safari

My Life My Travels

China Diary

Calcuttascape: Musings of a Globetrotter

Bera Bond

Hindi

Aap Biti Jag Biti